PRAISE FOR *POSITIVE C*

MW01026899

"Positive Communication for Leaders is an active leadership approach that gives practical, research-backed strategies for becoming a positive leader. This book provides useful guidance and powerful inspiration for how to turn an aspiration to be a leader with beneficial impact into a reality."

—**Jane Dutton,** Robert L. Kahn Distinguished University Professor Emerita, University of Michigan, Ross School of Business, Center for Positive Organizations

"Radical global changes require new ways of connecting, and the practices in *Positive Communication for Leaders* have proven valuable with organizational leaders and in our global development work where we support communities in their own transformation."

— **Hilary Haddigan,** chief of mission effectiveness, Heifer International

"This is a fantastic book relevant to a time in organizations when high trust relationships are more important than ever. It will push you to reflect and grow with practical tips to create real change!"

— **Hollie Packman,** founder, Packman and Associates, Inc.

"It is normal to engage in conventional conversations, yet some people become skilled in creating conversations of high, mutual, influence and impact. When we meet them, we never forget them. This inspiring and practical book will teach you how to become an unforgettable practitioner of positive communication. It is a must read."

—**Robert E. Quinn,** Margaret Elliot Tracy Professor Emeritus, University of Michigan, Ross School of Business, Center for Positive Organizations

"Mirivel and Lyon have written one of the most significant books of the decade in the communication discipline. Easy to read and grasp, the book provides a practical road map for mastering the power of positive communication. Leaders and laypeople will find this book to be of immense value in how to live a life of deep meaning."

—**Arvind Singhal,** Marston Endowed Professor of Communication at The University of Texas at El Paso, William J. Clinton Distinguished Fellow at the Clinton School of Public Service at the University of Arkansas in Little Rock

"Positive Communication for Leaders is an easy and enjoyable read based on a clear and well thought out communication model. It takes a storytelling approach to show why who you are and how you connect with others is the cornerstone of leadership effectiveness. A great tool to assess and improve your communication and leadership skills and impact change."

— **Pete Tanguay,** president, Rock Pond Pros

"Manifesting model leadership through communication skill, this book is an essential resource for everyone interested in properly relating to others."

— **Allen Weiner,** managing director and founder, Communication Development Associates

Positive Communication for Leaders

Proven Strategies for Inspiring Unity and Effecting Change

Julien C. Mirivel
and
Alexander Lyon

ROWMAN & LITTLEFIELD
Lanham • Boulder • New York • London

Senior Acquisitions Editor: Natalie Mandziuk
Assistant Acquisitions Editor: Yu Ozaki
Sales and Marketing Inquiries: textbooks@rowman.com

Credits and acknowledgments for material borrowed from other sources, and reproduced with permission, appear on the appropriate pages within the text.

Published by Rowman & Littlefield
An imprint of The Rowman & Littlefield Publishing Group, Inc.
4501 Forbes Boulevard, Suite 200, Lanham, Maryland 20706
www.rowman.com

86-90 Paul Street, London EC2A 4NE

British Library Cataloguing in Publication Information Available

Library of Congress Cataloging-in-Publication Data

978-1-5381-6760-1 (cloth)
978-1-5381-6761-8 (paperback)
978-1-5381-6762-5 (electronic)

Library of Congress Control Number: 20239408

∞™ The paper used in this publication meets the minimum requirements of American National Standard for Information Sciences—Permanence of Paper for Printed Library Materials, ANSI/NISO Z39.48-1992.

Contents

Preface

In a recent story that has gone viral, a soccer superstar explained the relationship he shares with his coach. The player, Antoine Griezmann, said the following about manager Didier Deschamps: "I owe him everything. I give everything for France, for the shirt, but also for him." He added, "Every move I make, every game I play is like a 'thank you' that I am sending him."[1]

We want the people you lead to feel the same way about you. We wrote this book to equip you—and other people who are in positions of leadership and influence—to create meaningful and influential relationships with your employees and have the skills to build a positive workplace culture.

A paradigm shift is taking place across organizations and contexts. People are no longer willing to work in an environment where they will be treated poorly, used, or abused. Employees today expect to feel valued and respected. They want to develop and grow professionally and be part of a positive culture.

The rapid development and use of technology and the global pandemic have made this more challenging. In 2018, for example, only approximately 5.7 percent of employees in the United States worked remotely on a full-time basis. By 2022 that percentage had jumped to 26 percent.[2] The vast majority of employees now work remotely at least some of the time. Some occupations and entire organizations are now entirely remote.

We recently held a leadership retreat for an organization that is now fully remote, with employees across the world working on projects together. As people gathered in the same space, they began to realize how much they had missed human contact. One person reflected: "I learned that we all used to take personal contact for granted. Remote work is good but it removes the social connection, which is what makes work more engaging and fun. . . . The power of interpersonal relationships is what matters." We couldn't agree more. These challenges call on leaders to find creative ways to bring people together and build connections.

Leaders today will need to connect more deeply with their employees and create an environment in which people from all walks of life can work together effectively, thrive as individuals and groups, and ultimately achieve extraordinary results. We believe that the secret sauce for achieving success in this new type of leadership role is positive communication. Accordingly, this book will show you how to master the power of positive communication in your leadership role.

We wrote this book together to merge our personal strengths. We started as peers as doctoral students at the University of Colorado at Boulder. We then worked together as colleagues at the University of Arkansas at Little Rock, where we wrote academic articles together, played video games on late Friday afternoons, and became good friends. To this book, Julien brings his passion for using the power of communication to connect more deeply with others. Through research, synthesis of communication theory, and personal experience, Julien developed a practical model of positive communication that is designed to help anyone communicate more effectively at work and at home. Alex brings expertise in organizational communication, leadership, and a focus on courageous communication in the workplace. The effectiveness of the model that frames this book has been tested by independent researchers and "road tested" with many clients from various organizations.

We also have practical leadership experience and know what it's like to be on the ground solving real problems. At his institution, Julien served as codirector of the academy of teaching and learning excellence, chairperson of a large academic department, associate dean, and dean of the college of social sciences and communication. Similarly, Alex served as chairperson of his department at SUNY Brockport and was the longtime director of his department's graduate program. We have both served as executive coaches, consultants, group facilitators, and speakers for local, national, and international organizations.

This book unites our areas of expertise to give you the best road map possible to communicate effectively and positively. Every chapter will equip you with the tools, techniques, and approaches you'll need to create high-quality connections, a thriving team, and a positive culture.

In another article about the French soccer manager Didier Deschamps, mentioned earlier, another star on the team praised his team manager. Olivier Giroud said, "What tips the balance is our team spirit." Another coach who'd worked for Deschamps in the past said, "His great strength is group cohesion." Still another player said, "He is clear in his speech and you can feel that there is a team in place."[3]

Most of us will never lead a national soccer team, but we can create the same lasting impact on the people we lead. Take a moment to read again what those around him said about Deschamps as a leader and then answer this question: What would your employees say about you and your leadership?

If you practice what you read in this book, you will accomplish what may seem impossible. You will unite your team, improve group cohesion, and create meaningful relationships. On that journey, we wish you the very best.

1

Positive Communication for Leaders

A vice president in an engineering firm called us. "I am in a tight spot," he said. "I have a great team, and we are performing at an all-time high. But I am losing the support of the board. I've made a few mistakes and even a few enemies. I've got three strikes against me, but I want to turn it all around."

He asked, "How can I get back on track and renew strained relationships with key stakeholders?"

The head of a large department was thrilled about the opportunity to move across the country for a new leadership role. Her excitement vanished when she got there. "I need your help," the new director explained. "My department is a hostile environment. People don't listen to one another. There's a great divide, and people are unhappy and unwilling to engage."

She asked, "What can I do to start creating positive change?"

A director from a large international travel firm was struggling. The pandemic forced the organization to restructure. Colleagues were fired. Morale was at an all-time low, and employee turnover was making it difficult to gain any forward momentum.

The director wanted to know, "How can we turn our team around?"

These are real, complex questions that demand practical solutions. They cut across the business sector, the public and nonprofit world, and higher education. The solution is the same. Each of these leaders will need to rise to the occasion and aspire to higher levels of excellence. Their success will depend on whether they are able to communicate effectively and positively.

Whether you are a new supervisor seeking to hone your skills, a manager leading a small group, or an executive overseeing large operations, you are in a leadership role because you want to make a greater impact. If you are like the many leaders we have met, you want to create a great culture in which people feel valued *and* achieve extraordinary results. You want to support your employees *and* keep them engaged. You need to lead meetings that are productive and enjoyable *and* produce a positive climate for all. You know what you need to do, but you may not know how to get there yet. In this book you will learn how through the power of positive communication.

***Positive communication will amplify your influence
and impact immediately.***

Developing your communication skills will amplify your leadership influence. We provide a practical guide to improve how you approach interaction, lead initiatives to reach critical goals, and manage your workplace culture. We share the techniques and the skills you will need to unify your team and effect real change. We will introduce our approach very soon. But before we do, take a moment to pause and reflect on a leader who has truly inspired you in box 1.1.

Box 1.1. **Your Most Inspirational Leader**

Instructions: Think about one of the most inspirational leaders for whom you have ever worked. Develop a solid picture of who they are. Now, recall what it was like to work with and for them.

- What emotions did they bring out of you?
- What did they do to make you feel this way?
- What aspect of their leadership style encouraged excellence in you?
- What were their habits, their personality traits, and their core behaviors?

Using a journal or a notepad, write down your answers to these questions. Reflect on the specific communication behaviors that made that person an inspiring leader.

Our goal is to help you create the same degree of inspiration in your employees that you experienced with this leader.

We cannot see your notes or know the person who inspired you in box 1.1. But we are willing to predict that your inspirational leader fits the following description:

√ They made you feel valued and respected.
√ They created an environment in which you were able to thrive.
√ They were fair and just when dealing with people, policies, expectations, and actions.
√ They created a great place to work, an environment that was challenging, encouraging, and safe.

In short, they were a positive leader. They made choices about how to be and how to act, and cultivated the conditions for an extraordinary workplace. They were a role model, a positive leadership example to look up to. You can become one too. But you need to be clear about your commitments.

ESTABLISH YOUR COMMITMENTS

How can leaders create a great place to work? What can leaders do to inspire people to great performance and higher career satisfaction while meeting their bottom line?

In recent years, researchers in the field of business have been trying to answer these questions. They have made great strides in pinpointing what great organizations are like and the types of leaders who create them.[1] Kim Cameron, a leader in this field, developed an approach called "positive leadership," which is designed to do just that.[2] Positive leadership not only "feels right" but is also backed up by scientific data and produces excellent results (as you will see throughout these chapters).

According to Cameron, positive leadership "aims not just to create positive emotions in people—to help people feel happy—but to dramatically affect organizational performance for the better."[3] The focus of this approach, then, is not just a feel-good, happy-go-lucky form of leadership. Its focus is on altering performance by allowing individuals and groups to achieve objectives and goals that are well above the norm. To do so, you'll need to approach leadership with at least three overlapping commitments.

Commitment 1: A Commitment to Excellence

A positive leader's first commitment is to excellence. Extraordinary leaders use their energy, their actions, and their behaviors to stretch the organization toward aspiring virtues. They use "intentional behaviors that depart from the norm . . . in *honorable ways*."[4] In contrast, a *poor* organization would be unprofitable, ineffective, or unethical. An *average* organization might be profitable, efficient, and even reliable. But *extraordinary* leaders achieve a state far beyond the norm: They transform the organization toward better values. They move the organization from being profitable to being generous. They move a system from being effective to being excellent. And they move the culture from a state of health to a state of vitality and flow.[5]

Extraordinary leaders use their energy, their actions, and their behaviors to stretch the organization toward aspiring virtues.

Commitment 2: A Commitment to Bringing Out People's Best

The second commitment is to approach the role with a firm belief in human capacity and potential. Positive leaders focus on strengths, not just development areas; discover what is right rather than strictly focusing on what is wrong; and inspire others. They bring with them a higher degree of optimism, conviction, strength, and hope for the future (see box 1.2). When leaders are encouraging, generous, just, and kind, they allow others to thrive. Great leaders help people go far beyond what they may believe they are capable of achieving. They help followers both perform at their best and also be the best versions of themselves as people. "The good of man," Aristotle wrote, "is a working of the soul in the way of excellence."[6] Positive leaders thus must be committed to bringing out people's best.

Commitment 3: A Commitment to Long-Term Investment in Others

Positive leaders are in it for the long run. Great leaders know there are no meaningful "quick fixes," "tricks," or "hacks" that will make a lasting difference. The trouble is, everywhere we look nowadays, somebody is selling instant results. But leadership is ultimately all about the people we lead. Positive change takes time because relationships take time. Results will rarely be

Box 1.2. **Your Most Inspirational Leader**

Instructions: Bring back to mind the person who inspired you. Check any of the following items that apply to their leadership approach:

☐ Did they demonstrate a commitment to excellence?
☐ Did they encourage you to become a better version of yourself?
☐ Did they take a long-term view of your development and success?

If your inspirational leader earned a check mark for any or all of those items, they embraced the nature of positive leadership. You can too.

immediate. That's why positive leaders must take a long-term view of success. As the old expression goes, "Rome wasn't built in a day." The research, tips, and advice you'll learn here can certainly be put into practice immediately, but achieving lasting results requires patience. Commit to making long-term investments in yourself, others, and your team. Commit to changing the way you approach human communication.

CHOOSE POSITIVE COMMUNICATION

A clear leadership philosophy is not enough. Our intentions may be great and our commitments strong, but what ultimately matters in leadership is what we do. It's the way you interact with the cleaning staff on a Friday afternoon. It's the phone call you make to an employee who lost a loved one. It's the encouraging note you send out to your team to inspire their best performance. It's the way you respond to an unexpected crisis.

What ultimately matters in leadership is not what you think or how you feel, it's what you do.

To create real change, you must turn your philosophical commitments into concrete actions. You have to walk the talk. That means the most pressing question is not "Do you *want* to be a positive leader?" The real question is "What can you actually *do* to lead more effectively and positively?"

In his work, Cameron explained that positive leadership depends on four interrelated elements.[7] The first is a positive climate, the creation of an environment in "which positive emotions predominate over negative emotions." The second is positive relationships, or the development of high-quality connections.[8] The third is positive meaning, or the feeling that one's work is aligned with a larger purpose or mission. The last element is *positive communication*. That's the focus of this book.

We argue that positive communication is at the heart of positive leadership. It is the central element that you need to master that connects to all others. When you practice it effectively, it will transform who you are as a professional and create a wave of influence over the teams and organizations you lead.

There is a significant body of research that documents the many benefits leaders get by using positive communication. Leaders who communicate positively gain the following:[9]

√ Create more encouraging working relationships with employees.
√ Increase employees' emotional attachment to the organization.
√ Increase employees' confidence in their ability to complete tasks.
√ Encourage employees to voluntarily address or prevent workplace problems.
√ Promote employee self-determination.

√ Boost employee motivation and commitment.
√ Promote greater satisfaction with direct reports and employee satisfaction in general.
√ Increase perceptions of fair treatment.
√ Enhance productivity.
√ Strengthen reputation as a more effective leader overall.

In addition to this list of benefits, people who practice positive communication are generally happier and promote similar personal well-being in their employees. Positive leaders create a more compassionate workplace, which increases the experience of positive emotions and reduces anxiety in others.[10]

If you put into practice what you read, you will grow as a person and a professional and immediately improve your communication. Over time you'll create more meaningful relationships with your team and your direct reports. You'll lead others more effectively. You'll cultivate a productive organizational culture in which your employees can thrive. You'll exceed your bottom line. As Cameron explained, "What people *give* to a relationship rather than what they *receive* from a relationship accounts for the positive effects."[11] To move in that direction, however, you need a reliable compass to point the way. That's what we offer next.

When you improve your communication, you naturally improve your relationships, the work climate, and what people experience.

YOUR COMPASS

Most professionals agree that communication is a crucial leadership skill. Still, it's difficult to determine what that means in practice. Deciding *how* to communicate is not always easy. We often do not know what to say, what to do, or how to approach a variety of situations. That's why we need a compass: to remind us of the direction we need to take.

Our compass is the "Wheel of Positive Communication," which Julien developed (see figure 1.1).[12] The wheel is a practical model of positive communication designed to help leaders communicate more effectively. The model identifies key communication behaviors that exemplify what leaders do when they are at their best. It captures small, concrete actions that you can take to create a positive and measurable impact. And it focuses on behaviors that are totally within your control and lead to transformative outcomes.

The model synthesizes decades of research across fields of study, draws on original interviews with communication experts, and has been "road-tested" with professionals across industry settings. The model's six core behaviors are proven to make a real difference for leaders. They are greeting, asking, complimenting, disclosing, encouraging, and listening.[13] These are small actions that have a big impact. Each communication practice is grounded in an easy-to-remember core principle that calls on leaders to elevate the way they engage with others. We explain each component with more detail later in this chapter.

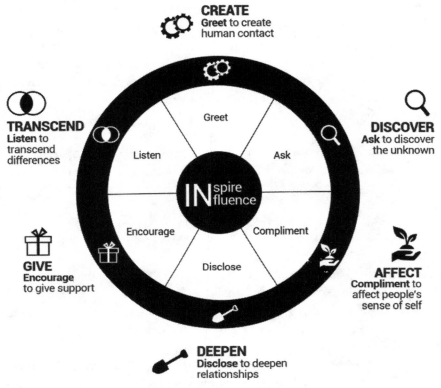

Figure 1.1. The Wheel of Positive Communication

Research shows that using the "Wheel of Positive Communication" creates tangible results. For example, one study found that the behaviors in the model account for over 97 percent of the transformational conversations that people experience.[14] Another study, led by Maryam Biganeh and Stacy Young and published in the *International Journal of Business Communication*, found that mastering the six positive communication behaviors was critical to both task-oriented leaders and relationship-oriented leaders, the two dominant leadership styles people typically choose.[15] Their findings showed that people in all walks of life respond positively when their leaders practice these six behaviors. There was also absolutely no difference between participants' race, gender, or age, showing that a leader's positive communication is valued by all. The authors concluded the following:

- "[P]ositive communication taps into the fundamental interpersonal attributes that everyone desires regardless of background . . . [and] serves as a foundational mechanism to create connection."[16]
- "Mirivel's model of positive communication has wide-reaching applicability in a diverse workforce . . . [and provides] actionable training methods designed to guide the ways in which leaders engage with employees, foster and strengthen relationships, and create cohesion in diverse work groups."[17]

Let's unpack our compass together piece by piece. The model begins on top and moves clockwise. Consider the following summary of what you will learn in each chapter:

CREATE
Greet to create human contact

The first behavior is the act of greeting. Greeting acknowledges that other people exist and naturally moves us in the direction of others. As a leader, you need to create lots of connections with people and be able to repair relationships when they are not doing well. When you master the act of greeting, you will create and expand relationships. *When you choose to greet others, you create human connections* (see chapter 2).

The second behavior is the act of asking questions. The questions you ask will shape the answers you get. As a leader, then, you need to place yourself in a position to discover what you do not know to better support the people you lead. *When you choose to ask open, meaningful questions, you discover the unknown* (see chapter 3).

DISCOVER
Ask to discover the unknown

AFFECT
Compliment to affect people's sense of self

The third behavior is the act of complimenting. What you say and do shapes not just who you are but how other people fundamentally see themselves. As a leader, you can use the power of communication to affect others. *When you choose to compliment, you will affect not only who people are in the moment but also who they become* (see chapter 4).

DEEPEN
Disclose to deepen
relationships

The fourth behavior is the act of disclosing. Disclosure occurs anytime you reveal something personal to others. It includes a leader's ability to be transparent, to share knowledge, and to express gratitude. *When you choose to disclose, you are deepening your relationships* (see chapter 5).

GIVE
Encourage
to give support

The fifth behavior is encouraging. Every workplace faces challenges. Every person needs support. Leadership is both managing organizational crises and finding ways to motivate and encourage employees. *When you choose to encourage, you are using communication as a gift and providing the necessary social support people need to succeed* (see chapter 6).

TRANSCEND
Listen to
transcend
differences

The sixth behavior is listening. At the personal level, leaders need to learn and practice deep listening. At the organizational level, they need to make sure that employees feel heard. In today's climate, more than ever, leaders need to listen to overcome the differences that exist between people. *When you choose to listen deeply, you will transcend the perceived differences between you and others* (see chapter 7).

Individually, each communication practice can make a difference at any given moment. When you practice all of them consistently and holistically, you become a positive leader (see box 1.3). Mastering the art of positive communication will help you achieve what may seem impossible: You can *influence and inspire* your team for greatness. We use this compass to level up your leadership game.

How many check marks did your inspirational leader earn in our survey in box 1.3? Given the results, did they practice positive communication? If so, you have an easy road map to aspire to. Now it's your turn to practice the art of positive communication and be an inspirational role model to others.

LEVEL UP YOUR COMMUNICATION

The chapters that follow take you through all six positive leadership practices and show you how to put them into action in your professional life. Each chapter unpacks one core principle in four major sections to help you level up your skills.

Box 1.3.   **How Did Your Inspirational Leader Communicate?**

Instructions: Two researchers we mentioned, Biganeh and Young, developed a short survey to measure the impact of leaders' positive communication on employees.[1] Take a moment to review the questions below, which we have adapted. Think back to the leader who inspired you. To what extent did they practice positive communication? Check each item that applies.

☐ My inspirational leader regularly said "hello" or "good morning/afternoon" to me and created meaningful time to connect with me.

☐ My inspirational leader asked meaningful questions to help me consider new ways of approaching my job and frequently sought to understand my position.

☐ My inspirational leader gave me positive feedback about my performance.

☐ My inspirational leader disclosed personal information about their past experiences and expressed gratitude.

☐ My inspirational leader expressed confidence in my abilities and recognized my accomplishments.

☐ My inspirational leader listened to me and others deeply.

☐ My inspirational leader inspired me to do my best.

Note

1. Biganeh, M., & Young, S. L. (2021). Followers' perceptions of positive communication practices in leadership: What matters and surprisingly what does not. *International Journal of Business Communication.* https://doi.org/10.1177%2F2329488420987277

Level 1 introduces you to the basics of the behavior and how to use its power. At this level, we show you how to quickly implement the behavior and see tangible results in your one-on-one interactions.

Level 2 takes it up a step. We show you how to draw on the behavior to reach group-level impact and expand your thinking to become more productive. At level 2, you will make a paradigm shift in your leadership approach.

Level 3 is designed to implement the behavior at the team and organizational level. As a leader, you have to think both about the small microbehaviors that shape your interactions with others and the long-term strategies and initiatives you implement. You need to expand your efforts to reach all stakeholders because your energy alone will not be sufficient to affect a whole culture. Level 3 therefore shows how to tap into the power of positive communication to develop organizational initiatives and strategies that will expand your realm of influence.

Level 4 is about turning what you've learned into action. That means you'll put the information you've read into daily practice. We wrap up every chapter with a quick summary of the major takeaways and encourage you to choose the next steps you need to succeed.

AN INVITATION

This book is designed to be your guide to the art of positive communication for leaders. We designed it to combine practical and research-driven suggestions to implement the "Wheel of Positive Communication" in your leadership approach. You'll hear numerous stories and examples from professionals who have tested these strategies and had a positive impact in their workplaces. At the end (see chapter 8), you will draft a concrete communication plan to put it all into practice.

Positive leaders offer much more than a superficial sunny disposition. As we mentioned at the opening of the chapter, leaders face seemingly endless challenges every day. Leaders have to find ways to renew strained relationships, create positive moments when things are stuck, and set the right tone amid ever-increasing turbulence and stress. As the fictional boxer Rocky Balboa once said, "Let me tell you something you already know. The world ain't all sunshine and rainbows." Any leader who's been on the job more than 24 hours understands this. Complex problems demand practical solutions. People look to their leaders to show them the way forward. As an excellent leader, you must make small but crucial decisions about how you lead and how you communicate. As you'll learn in the next chapter, those small choices begin right at the start of interaction, with greetings.

2

Greet to Create Human Contact

"Connor," a young professional, was recently telling us about his first few days at a new job. He met the night manager near the end of his second day. The manager paused to say "Hello," introduced himself, and asked for Connor's name. The manager then said simply, "I appreciate all the hard work that you have been doing."

"This made me feel like I can do it here. All I have ever wanted since I started working is to be somewhere I know I can be the best me possible." This greeting, he added, gave him "a confidence boost and a feeling of fulfillment. . . . If I ever get to the position where I am over many individuals, I will be sure to say small things because it can really make a person's day."

Positive communication has a powerful influence even in brief conversations like this one. The opening moments of an interaction are rich and meaningful opportunities for leaders. A good greeting begins with the intention to move toward others, narrow the gap, and invite a connection. The act of greeting others well is a skill you need to establish positive connections and ultimately expand your influence. Consider these questions as an informal self-assessment:

✓ Do you tend to take time to initiate contact with others, or do you rush from task to task?

✓ Do you move in the direction of others, or do you avoid social interaction?

✓ Are you fully present when you interact with others, or do you come across as preoccupied?

Keep your answers in mind. In this chapter you'll learn the first principle of positive communication for leaders: **when you greet, you create a human connection**.

You'll work on three related greeting skills. First, we focus on the power of opening a connection with others. Greetings serve critical functions and help leaders form a positive team culture. Second, you'll learn to see communication as an act of creation. What you experience with others is not predetermined; it is always under construction. It is a fully dynamic process that you can shape through your communication. Third, you'll learn to encourage real connections across your organization and create a meaningful network of relationships. Finally, we distill the key takeaways you can put into practice today.

LEVEL 1: THE POWER OF GREETINGS

When you greet another, you acknowledge that the other person exists and is worthy of your attention. A greeting says, "*I see you. I acknowledge you. I know you are there.*" And although it might seem trivial, taking the time and initiative to greet somebody with care begins the process of connection and starts conversations on the right foot.

Greetings play a pivotal role in interaction because they set in motion what is to come next. They lead to a response. "Hey, good morning," you might say to one of your staff members on Monday morning. Because you have initiated the conversation, they are in a position to respond: "Hey, good morning. How are you?" And here it is. *Boom!* The opening of a conversation creates the opportunity for further connection. The moment we greet is the moment we enter the realm of relationships.

Greetings can last mere seconds or begin an extended conversation, but they are never insignificant. They accomplish a number of important functions for leaders:

1. **Greetings open a sequence of communication between two people.** As long as one person makes the first move, the sequence for communication has started, and connection has begun.
2. **Greetings both define and affirm people and their relationships.** The moment you initiate and say "Hello," you are demonstrating that you are engaged, are approachable, and care about others. This is one reason employees who have the least resources or power feel so rewarded when high-level company leaders notice and greet them personally.
3. **Greetings serve as a bridge to achieve a specific purpose.** When we greet people in professional settings, a greeting is not just about making social contact. We are also politely positioning ourselves to collaborate. In conversations, we expect that a greeting is just the beginning.

Studies show that greetings matter across virtually all cultures and workplace contexts. For example, in the world of education, researchers have shown that students learn more and perform better when instructors start class with a warm greeting.[1] Warm greetings from teachers also impact student retention and parental involvement.[2] In the world of medicine, the single most consequential sign of disrespect that patients experience occurs when physicians do not greet them personally when they walk into the room. Skipping the greeting substantially decreases patients' satisfaction, trust in their physician, and the likelihood they will follow the doctor's recommended treatment.[3] In the context of selling, we know that greeting customers warmly and appropriately boosts sales.[4] Greetings also matter in the context of leadership. As author Jon Gordon explained, "Connection and relationship are what drive real growth" and in "order to connect with others, you have to be someone who creates connections."[5] In this section, we focus on four critical leadership habits that will help you create connections.

Habit 1: Initiate the Greeting and Build Relationships

The first leadership habit is initiating contact. It's about putting yourself in a physical and relational position to start the conversation.

Although it appears easy to do, initiating contact is fraught with tension. Leaders can sometimes stall or avoid greetings, especially when managing difficult tasks and responsibilities. We get busy and preoccupied with the task at hand. Some people experience social anxiety to a degree that makes greetings difficult. And many people also have a natural tendency to wait for others to acknowledge them or greet them first—mostly driven by our fundamental need to feel loved, valued, and respected. Initiating interaction takes more effort and involves risk. After all, many of us feel much more comfortable being acknowledged rather than doing the acknowledging. By initiating interaction, you are moving from passively wanting to feel respected to showing others that you respect them.

When you initiate an interaction, you move from passively wanting to feel respected to **showing** *others that you respect them.*

Consider this story about the power and pivotal role of greetings. Several years ago, Julien and a colleague welcomed fifteen students from Pakistan to Little Rock, Arkansas. Prior to coming to the United States, the students' perceptions of American culture and its people were mostly negative. The students said that they thought Americans were "rude," "ill-mannered," aggressive," or even "cruel." "My perception," one person explained, "was that America and Americans want our destruction." Another participant didn't think Americans would "even like to talk to us." He explained, "I thought that all Americans hate us." With this understanding and context, Julien and his colleague wondered how to begin the first meeting with these students. How could they welcome them into a completely new culture and shift their perceptions?

On the first day they began the session by greeting the students warmly in their native language. They bowed from a distance and welcomed them with the phrase "Assalamu-akeykum." This is a traditional Arabic greeting that means "May peace be upon you." The students' reaction was warm and noticeably positive. They then each proceeded to teach the next response: "Waleykum-salaam," or "Peace be upon you also." That moment of politeness was a turning point for the students.

In follow-up research conducted by Derek Wingfield, he found that the students not only remembered the greeting with fondness; they saw it as a transformative moment.[6] Their perceptions of American culture and its people also shifted. "When asked to describe Americans following their visit to the U.S.," Wingfield wrote, "the students called [Americans] 'candid,' 'peace-loving,' and 'great and good human beings.'" One participant explained: "They have a great respect for humanity. . . . America is a country where people from any country and culture can live happily without having any discrimination." All of the students' mindsets about American culture had changed in a positive direction. This transformation started with the decision to make a clear, positive move by initiating a greeting in their native tongue. See box 2.1 for help with common international greetings.

Box 2.1. **Learn to Greet in Multiple Languages**

Many organizations today operate in locations around the world. Hone your greeting skills by learning to start interaction in languages commonly spoken for business. It is particularly important to make this effort when visiting international professionals in their home countries, but it can come in handy in many situations. Use your own best judgment about when greetings like these would be most appropriate.

- Chinese: Start with "Ni Hao" to say hello or add "Ni Hao Ma" to say "Hello, how are you?"
- Spanish: Keep it simple, with "Hola" or "Buenos dias," and then add "Como estas," which means "How are you?"
- Arabic: The traditional greeting in Arabic is "Assalamu-Aleykum." You can say it just like you read it. If someone else speaks first, respond with "Waleykum-Salam."
- French: Begin with "Bonjour" and a friendly smile.
- German: Start the interaction with "Guten tag" and end with "Auf wiedersehen." Prounce this as "owf vee-der-say-en."
- Portuguese: The easy way to start is to say "Bom Dia" (spoken as "Bon Gia") with excitement and joy.

The simplest way for you to make contact, then, is to initiate the greeting. This is particularly important when beginning new leadership roles and for initial encounters. You need to move in the direction of others and find creative ways of connecting with people. Whether learning how to greet a client from Japan with warmth and politeness, shaking hands with every person in a meeting, or being intentional about your tone and warmth, these are the details that matter in the sea of relationships. And once you start an interaction, you have to be willing to make time for the other person.

Habit 2: Make Time for Connection

As busy as working life is for many leaders, great leaders take the time to not only greet and welcome interaction but also use the opening to create quality moments. Our second habit is about creating time and space in your day for connection.

For decades now, Janet Holmes and Maria Stubbe from the University of Wellington in New Zealand have been collecting data across almost a dozen workplaces to study how people talk at work.[7] They have recorded thousands of hours of conversations. They put small audio recorders in formal and informal meeting spaces, like near drinking fountains, in cafeterias, and in individuals' offices. They then transcribed all of the conversations and analyzed the data.

The most significant finding from New Zealand's Language in the Workplace Project (LWP) is this: small talk at work matters. People give updates about families, make disclosures of personal challenges, crack funny jokes, offer comments about their weekend, or ask a question about how another person is doing. Those are the conversations that really matter in the workplace. This is one important way people build a sense of collegiality, get to know one another, and weave the fabric of the organization's culture. When small talk is present, *it oils the social wheels*. But when it's absent, it's a huge red flag.[8]

One implication of this study is that to foster a great culture, leaders need to create lots of moments for connections with others. In other words, leaders need to see good greetings, small talk, and building relationships as an everyday responsibility. No one is better at this than our friend Rob.

Robert Ulmer is dean of the Greenspun College of Urban Affairs at the University of Nevada at Las Vegas. Originally from Canada, Rob brings enthusiasm, positivity, and a full commitment to people—all day, every day. In fact, both of us have experienced Rob in the same way when he served as our chairperson. When we walked into his office, Rob would instantly let go of whatever he was doing, turn to us with a warm greeting, and give us his undivided attention. We also cannot recall a single instance when we felt pushed out, nudged to leave, or disengaged. Rob gives you his full self. So we asked him how he does it in a recent interview.

"As a leader, I have to be sensitive to the human equation," Rob explained on a Zoom call. "People really do matter to me," he added. "You're hiring people and you have to give them time and attention. You have to be interested in who they are and what they're about. You have to care."

"People," he explained, "signal to you whether you matter or not, whether they are more interested in you or more interested in themselves." He took a brief pause and then added: "I know what that feeling is like and I don't want them to have that feeling."

"The default for most people," Rob said, "is to be impersonal. Many people will treat others transactionally. It's very easy to focus on the role and the position and everybody will tell you that you can't take the time to spend with people, that it's about something else." He paused for clarity. "That's all nonsense," he said as he shook his head. "Investing in relationships can be done at all leadership levels."

In the interview, Alex stepped in and played devil's advocate: "I can imagine people saying, 'I can't do that all the time. I've got emails to attend to, another meeting to go to.'" Alex listed all the things that could take a person away from the encounter. Rob responded, "So my question is, out of all of the things that you've listed, what could be more important than the person you have with you in that moment?"

This moment reveals the mindset that drives Rob's approach to work. As he put it in the interview, "relationships are the most important priority." There is nothing above that. From his vantage point, there is no internal leadership conflict about his priorities. He is living his principles. "I am not using a focus on relationships as a way to get to some other outcome," Rob concluded. "The end outcome is the relationship."

With this philosophy in mind, Rob makes lots of small and big decisions that bring to life this philosophy. Rob is a master at creating and maintaining relationships. At one point in the conversation, he reflected, "Sure, we have a whole bunch of problems today. We'll have them tomorrow. I don't go into work with the expectation that I'm going to have a perfect day. So, when I'm talking to people, I go in and have those meaningful conversations for as long as it takes. Those other extraneous issues don't really matter. What gets us where we're going in the long run is the relationships that we're developing." See box 2.2 for a list of Rob's daily concrete habits.

Rob's approach to leadership echoes one of the most significant lessons from the Harvard Grant Study.[9] Started more than seventy-five years ago, the Harvard Grant Study explored the lives of 261 individuals throughout their lifespans. Researchers began with surveys and in-depth interviews and then collected data throughout each person's adult life from their twenties through their thirties, forties, and fifties, and ultimately in their eighties and

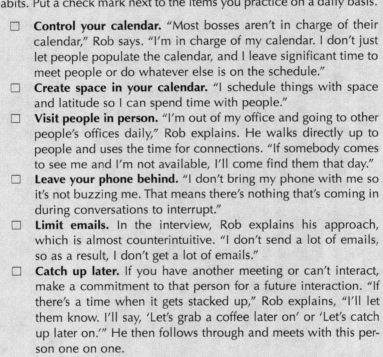

Box 2.2.   **How Can I Make Time and Space for Quality Connection?**

Instructions: Following are several practical suggestions with illustrative examples from our interview with Rob. He practices all of these habits. Put a check mark next to the items you practice on a daily basis.

☐ **Control your calendar.** "Most bosses aren't in charge of their calendar," Rob says. "I'm in charge of my calendar. I don't just let people populate the calendar, and I leave significant time to meet people or do whatever else is on the schedule."

☐ **Create space in your calendar.** "I schedule things with space and latitude so I can spend time with people."

☐ **Visit people in person.** "I'm out of my office and going to other people's offices daily," Rob explains. He walks directly up to people and uses the time for connections. "If somebody comes to see me and I'm not available, I'll come find them that day."

☐ **Leave your phone behind.** "I don't bring my phone with me so it's not buzzing me. That means there's nothing that's coming in during conversations to interrupt."

☐ **Limit emails.** In the interview, Rob explains his approach, which is almost counterintuitive. "I don't send a lot of emails, so as a result, I don't get a lot of emails."

☐ **Catch up later.** If you have another meeting or can't interact, make a commitment to that person for a future interaction. "If there's a time when it gets stacked up," Rob explains, "I'll let them know. I'll say, 'Let's grab a coffee later on' or 'Let's catch up later on.'" He then follows through and meets with this person one on one.

nineties. The research is still ongoing, as many participants are still leading healthy and productive lives. George Vaillant, who served as director of the study for over forty years, was interviewed after publishing a summary of the core findings in his book *Triumphs of Experience*. In one article, the reporter asked: "What have you been learning from collecting all of this data on people's lives?" Vaillant replied: "It's quite simple really. The only thing that really matters in life are the relationships that you have with other people."[10] We believe this is true of leadership too.

Positive leaders draw on the fundamental understanding that *leadership is relationship*. It is based in the process of initiating contact with people, getting to know them, enjoying those interactions, and being fully present with them. Saying hello, catching up with people, sharing jokes, and updating others about our lives collectively weave the fabric of our relationships, create mutual understanding, and increase our positive leadership influence. Still, you have to learn to pay attention to the details to greet people well.

Leadership is relationship.

Habit 3: Open Interactions with Care

If you are going to greet others, you might as well do it with care and attention. The New Zealand Language at Work Project revealed that small details in greetings can tell you a lot about a leader or organization. For example, if small talk is common in a workplace, there's a high likelihood of collegiality, positiveness, and employee satisfaction. If small talk is not common, it can be a red flag that the organization and its people are not doing well.[11]

Imagine visiting an organization, for instance. When you walk in, there is a person at the front desk smiling and welcoming you. "Good morning," he says warmly, "how can I help you?" You explain the reason for your visit and he asks you to sit. "May I get you a bottle of water or coffee?" he asks. You say "No, thank you," but you're impressed by his thoughtful attention. You sit down to wait for the visit. Meanwhile, you see people interacting and laughing with one another. People are clearly working, but there is a sense of support, enjoyment, and flow. When the person you're visiting comes to meet you, you notice the same thing. There is a smile, a welcoming demeanor, and a handshake. "It's so nice to meet you," she says, "I've been looking forward to connecting with you." This organization marinates its greetings with care.

Now imagine walking into a second organization. When you arrive, there is someone at the front desk. You step through the front door, but no one says "hello." Instead, an employee approaches you and skips straight to "How can I help you?" He asks the question with an annoyed tone as if you've interrupted his morning. You see no smile and sense no warmth. "Please sit here," he says, "I'll call her in." While you wait, all you can hear is the sound of the air conditioner buzzing. There are no interactions taking place. You hear no laughter, engagement, or friendly conversations. A few minutes later, the

CEO comes in to meet you. "Good morning," she says with a degree of stress in her voice, "I have about thirty minutes, so let's get started."

Technically speaking, you were greeted in both scenarios. But the details create contrasting experiences that reveal much about each organization. The presence or absence of certain features like care, warmth, and attention shape how people feel about one another and influence the conversation that follows. It even makes a difference in email communications. See box 2.3 for a list of greeting fundamentals.

Box 2.3.   Good Greeting Checklist

Instructions: Use this checklist to create positive greetings for when you see people at work for the first time each day. Imagine how these communication behaviors would look and sound in an ideal conversation. Use the checklist to role-play a few greetings right now.

- √   Prepare yourself to communicate with an attitude of kindness.
- √   Use words that greet: "Hi," "Hello," "Good morning," "Good afternoon."
- √   Use the person's name: "Hi, Sam."
- √   Ask a question to show interest and demonstrate politeness: "How are you?" "How was your weekend?"
- √   Show warmth: use a friendly smile, attentive eye contact, and an affirming head nod.
- √   Allow an extra minute or two for small talk.

Habit 4: Start and Finish Your Emails Thoughtfully

In addition to the importance of small talk, the LWP in New Zealand showed that details in the way people write and read emails matter. In one study, for example, researchers found that even though almost all professionals believe that starting and ending an email well is important, "over 60% of emails in the workplace begin without any formal greeting while another 25% started with the person's name only."[12]

In another study, led by Joan Waldvogel, researchers explored two very different organizations.[13] In the first organization, Company A, the study showed high levels of conflict, low employee morale, low satisfaction, and high employee turnover. The second organization, Company B, showed the opposite. It was an exemplary positive organization. There, people felt excited about the culture, celebrated one another's birthdays, and reported high levels of engagement and satisfaction, and the organization boasted both extraordinary results and very high rates of employee retention. Researchers then collected hundreds of emails across both organizations to analyze the patterns. When they looked for critical differences, they found something striking.

In Company A, where satisfaction was low and conflict high, most emails to individuals and groups looked like this:

Example 1

The meeting is at 5:00 p.m on Friday. John.

Example 2

The reports are due two weeks from today. Thanks. Julie.

In Company B, the organization exemplifying positive communication, the emails were about the same types of tasks, but the ways in which people engaged one another differed drastically. Consider the contrast:

Example 1

Hi everyone,
 I hope you are having a good day. Just a quick reminder that our meeting is scheduled for 5:00 p.m. on Friday. I look forward to seeing everyone there.
 Thanks all,
 John

Example 2

Hello everybody,
 Please remember that your reports are due two weeks from today. I know you've been working hard on these. I look forward to reading them and seeing your work. Thank you so much for everything you do.
 Julie

Can you see, hear, and feel the difference between the two sets of emails? The raw information in both sets of emails is essentially the same. In Company B, however, the authors of the emails include a greeting, some well wishes, encouraging words, and a warm conclusion. These emails, in other words, take the time, care, and attention to build and maintain relationships. As the researcher explained, "the much greater use made of greetings and closings in [the positive organization] suggests that staff members are concerned to establish a friendly tone in their interactions and maintain good interpersonal relationships."[14]

The members of both organizations are making small daily choices that have a huge impact. In the negative organization, people were focused on the basic message only and treated one another, as Rob Ulmer described earlier, in a *transactional* manner. The extra care and attention from employees of Company B helped create and maintain the close relationships people were experiencing and encouraged a positive culture. See box 2.4 for effective email strategies.

Whether or not you greet others thoughtfully, your communication choices matter. When you choose to open up conversation and greet others warmly, you naturally enter the realm of positive relationships. In this section, you have learned four leadership habits that are essential to create positive connections with others. We now take you to the next level by showing you that communication is not just a mode of transmitting information; it is an act of creation that forms the bonds you have with others.

LEVEL 2: CREATE MEANINGFUL RELATIONSHIPS

The act of greeting, as we argued earlier, is the first critical step leaders take to create a connection. In this section, we focus on how greetings will help you create meaningful relationships with others. We emphasize the word *create* because we want you to see and understand that communication is not just a mode of transmitting data. Many leaders mistakenly think that communicating well simply requires having a message to share, pressing send on your mailbox, or speaking up. Today, however, effective leaders and seasoned researchers know that communication is not just a way of transmitting information; it is a constitutive process by which relationships are created.[15] Communication is a dynamic process, as it forms and reshapes who we are, what our relationships are all about, and what our experiences with others are like.

Box 2.4. **Effective Strategies for Email**

Joan Waldvogel studied email communication in the workplace to understand patterns and practices that hinder communication, create miscommunication, or hurt relationships. She found that the following practices are critical to maintaining good working relationships:[1]

- Develop a short subject line that clearly identifies the topic.
- Make sure to include a warm greeting and a professional sign-off unless it is part of an ongoing dialogue.
- Write a message that is concise and to the point. In other words, keep your emails short. If you find yourself writing multiple paragraphs, make a phone call instead.
- Avoid the unnecessary use of capital letters, exclamation points, or any emphasis on words or phrases. These nonverbal signals can easily be interpreted as signs of anger or impatience.
- Use emoticons sparingly. Her research shows that most people don't like them.
- Use email for people you cannot reach physically. "People," she wrote, "do not appreciate being sent an email by someone who could easily pass on that message in person."
- Respond within 24 to 48 hours because almost "85 percent of those surveyed expected a response within one or two days."

Note

1. Waldvogel, J. (2002). Some features of workplace emails. *New Zealand English Journal*, 16, 42–52.

Your communication does not merely reflect your experience; it creates your experience.

Communication, then, is an act of creation. The message you send, the email you write, the posture you take during a meeting—all of those details communicate meaning about who you are, what you care about, and how you relate to others. Consider the following shift:

Communication as Transmission	*Communication as Creation*
• What message should I deliver? • What feedback should I give? • How do I respond?	• What experience do I want to create? • What does my communication style *reveal* about who I am? • What am I *doing* to initiate, build, and maintain positive relationships with others?

Although you may not be conscious or aware of all that you do, your small decisions, movements, tone, facial expressions, words, and other choices you make in conversations all shape the way others experience you. Thinking about communication as a *creative act* reminds you that you cannot escape the process of relating.

This was a lesson Alex learned early from his father. In his teenage years, Alex was a musician in a local rock band. To him, this was no hobby. He was serious about music and wanted to make a living working full-time as a professional just like his father. Perhaps he was too serious. He was hungry for success beyond measure, but his ambition came at a relational price. His musician friends started giving him consistent feedback that he was acting like a "jerk." He expressed himself too intensely. He was opinionated and overly task focused, to the point where fellow musicians no longer enjoyed working with him. Alex went to his father to explain what was going on and ask for advice. "I don't feel like a 'jerk,' but that's what they're saying." His father replied, "I know you're not a 'jerk.' I know who you are inside." His father took a long pause. "Still, if you're upsetting people with how you act on the outside, then their perceptions matter too. The way you handle yourself will have an influence. You have to decide what kind of influence you want to have."

As he thought about it, Alex saw that his anxiety and frustration about his lack of career progress was rubbing off on others. His highest priorities were working hard, working fast, and moving forward as quickly as possible. The way he talked to his fellow musicians was focused only on exchanging information as efficiently as possible. He didn't take the time to connect with, value, and enjoy the company of others, and they all noticed. The conversation with his father was a hard pill to swallow, but he also felt a sense of empowerment about how he could talk to people in the future. He had never even considered the way his communication influenced his relationships.

He realized he was not merely transmitting information, he was creating his social world.

What social world are you creating with your communication? Take a moment here to reflect on these questions:

- What aspects of your communication are hindering your ability to connect with others?
- What are other people signaling to you about your leadership approach and how they see you?
- What positive communication behaviors could make your interactions more authentic?

With these questions in mind, we now share three critical mindsets you can draw on to create and sustain more meaningful relationships with others.

Mindset 1: Create a Network of Connections

The first mindset is to create a network of new relational connections. The power of greetings lies in their function to begin the process of connection. Greetings can help you spark new relationships and sustain those that already exist. Relationship-building behaviors may feel counterintuitive to some leaders as they "move up."

As professionals move from individual contributor roles into leadership positions, some start to feel held back by their job titles or elevated positions. Other people notice. In an interview we conducted, author and consultant Allen Weiner explained it this way. "*Leaders occupy roles that seem to come with the prescription to act appropriately distant from followers,*" he said to start. "Many leaders feel as if they can't violate these expectations and that limits their choices. In contrast, *leaders who cultivate positive, dynamic conversations have created a 'crack,'* so to speak, in their prescribed role. Some high-level leaders, for instance, start conversations with individuals who were likely pleasantly surprised that the CEO was greeting them on a first-name basis. The fact is, the more we know about the people we interact with the less our prescribed role dominates the conversation."

As a leader, you need to hone your ability to start, cultivate, and expand a large network of professional relationships. You can do this in several ways:

√ **Initiate contact with already existing connections**. With so much at
   stake, we believe it's the leader's responsibility to initiate greetings and
   do their part to maintain meaningful relationships. When you arrive
   at work, take a moment to briefly drop by people's offices to open the
   lines of communication and affirm your existing relationships.

√ **Start new connections.** Take our greeting challenge by inviting new
   connections into the realm of your experience (see box 2.5). Schedule
   time to invite new people for coffee or lunch and slowly expand your
   network.

√ **Send an email to check in.** Most email communication in the workplace is used for two primary reasons: to give information or to make
   a request for information. Instead, use email communication to build
   and maintain relationships. For example, send an email to a colleague
   to check in on how they are doing—especially if you know they are
   facing a difficult time.

Our point is this: use the creative power of communication to cultivate a
network of meaningful relationships. Investing even a few minutes a day can
create major long-term relationship results.

Box 2.5.   **Greeting Challenge**

Instructions: It's time to start exercising your greeting muscles. Here is
your greeting challenge:

- Make a list of three individuals in your organization you do not
  know well.
- This week, make it a point to swing by their offices.
- Give them your best greeting and attempt to make a genuine
  connection.
- If you're feeling brave, set up a time to meet for coffee or lunch
  sometime soon.

Mindset 2: Avoid the Silent Treatment

It's up to you to get connections started despite the circumstances. In his first administrative role, Julien was asked to step in as director of an academic department that was highly dysfunctional. Although the department had long been a collegial space, it had become a hostile workplace environment. The negative energy was palpable as you stepped off of the elevator and entered the hallway. People would come to work, enter their offices, and close the door immediately. When they walked by other people's offices, not a word was uttered, not even a simple hello. Sometimes people even took the stairs from the back of the building to avoid randomly crossing paths with others. People were giving each other the silent treatment.

Quiet hostility can come from peers, but it often stems straight from the leader. Amy Morin, a writer for *Inc.* magazine, wrote that an astounding 64 percent of employees report getting the silent treatment at work.[16] She explained that the silent treatment is one of the top ways that employees experience workplace bullying. Most of the time, the person with more official authority, such as a supervisor, initiates the silent treatment. It is a form of quiet punishment that takes away the greeting as a first line of attack by refusing to interact with or even socially ostracizes peers or subordinates. Greetings are about connecting. So it's only natural that they would be the first aspect of communication to disappear when relationships are in trouble.

Remember, no matter what you do, you are creating your relationships for better or for worse. In other words, the silent treatment still sends a message whether we intend it to or not. When people withdraw, we give off a variety of cues that lead to conflict, confrontation, and awkwardness. For instance, we create more physical space between ourselves and others and make less eye contact. Our internal anxiety may cause our faces to tighten, our bodies to stiffen, and our attitude to show frustration. We are less likely to crack a joke or a smile. When we do speak, our messages are likely to be short, direct, and to the point rather than making polite requests or asking patient questions. Avoiding communication for too long creates a downward spiral of hostility. Avoiding others is not a healthy or effective default leadership strategy. It's the leader's job to connect.

Mindset 3: Restart the Connection after Conflicts

It's the leader's job to restart strained connections. Don't wait for others to take the first step. Several weeks ago, Alex had a trivial disagreement with his wife. The argument started small but then spiraled quickly. In the span of just a few minutes, Alex and his wife both felt misunderstood and hurt. Instead of resolving the issue or letting the conversation escalate further, they then did what most people do. They retreated to opposite ends of the house to cool off. This worked well for a while, until Alex heard his two dogs stirring outside. He decided to walk across the house to get to the back door in the kitchen. As he waited for the dogs to come inside, he heard another door open and some movement in the house. His wife was on the way to the kitchen. He now faced a choice. One option was to leave the kitchen awkwardly and pass his wife in silence while avoiding eye contact to return to his home office. The second, more courageous, option was to remain in the kitchen until his wife walked in and make the effort to greet her sincerely. He did the calculations and decided that the best option was to initiate a brief but positive interaction. When his wife arrived in the kitchen, Alex lifted his eyes, looked in her direction, and simply greeted her. She reciprocated with a quick hello, and the tension immediately started to fade.

This scenario is not unusual. Creating space or simply avoiding others is often an automatic response for managing conflict or everyday stress. It may feel natural to keep to ourselves or avoid a situation for a little while, but we can't allow this to become a long-term pattern. It's the leader's responsibility to restart connections when the situation has stalled. We lead relationships, not just organizations. We do this by setting the tone, making the first move, and doing our part to make things better.

It's the leader's responsibility to initiate connection and to restart connection following conflicts.

As mentioned earlier, Julien was asked to lead a department that had essentially become a hostile workplace environment. His purpose was simple: recreate the positive workplace culture the department had once had. In the first few weeks on the job, he immediately noticed numerous powerful negative communication behaviors during meetings. When faculty members stepped into the space, their bodies and faces became visibly tighter. People did not greet each other. They simply sat in their chairs when they arrived at meetings and seemed to wait for a moment to pounce on one another when one of them spoke. Some of the behaviors were also downright disrespectful. When a certain faculty member expressed their voice, a number of other faculty members immediately turned to their phones to text one another. Sometimes people smirked and laughed in a spirit of mockery. When conversations took place, people did not respect each other's voice, interrupted one another abruptly, or became excessively argumentative. People around the table used behaviors that created defensiveness:

- They made evaluative comments rather than descriptive ones.
- They were strategic by ganging up rather than being spontaneous with the natural flow of the conversation.
- They ignored others' comments or contributions rather than showing empathy and understanding.
- They used a voice of superiority and certainty in their views rather than communicating based on a premise of equality and flexibility.

In other words, their communication choices were recreating a negative, hostile, and defensive culture every single day.

The question for any leader in this position is this: What should I do to respond to help the department members reengage with each other more positively? How do I confront the problem without making it worse?

One of Julien's approaches was to meet with key individuals who seemed to be a primary source of the conflict. In one conversation, he set up an appointment with a faculty member in his office. He started with some small talk but quickly focused the conversation on some of the problematic behaviors he'd seen in meetings. "What you are doing here and now," he said, "is hurting other people and ultimately the department. Together, I know that we can create a much better workplace for all, but I need you to change your communication so that we can create it."

He was fairly direct, and the meeting did not go well. There were tears, the individual stormed out, and the meeting ended abruptly. Julien had to decide what to do next.

Although the first conversation did not go smoothly, Julien knew it was important to be consistent in his approach to the relationship and cue that the relationship would continue in the spirit of goodwill. This was not the end. It was simply the beginning of a larger conversation.

Given the nature of the conflict, Julien decided to allow for some temporary space and time for the other person to process the feedback he'd offered. His biggest challenge was deciding what to do next. Should Julien drop by and initiate small talk? Should he wait for the employee to make contact? Should it be done in person or via email?

In this case, Julien decided to move in the direction of the employee and reinitiate face-to-face contact. Walking through the hallway the next day, Julien swung by the person's office and said a quick "Hello." It was a brief interaction and designed to cue the continuation of the relationship. She reciprocated, and there was a visible sign of a brief smile. Slowly, day by day, the length of the interactions increased again, with periods of listening and dialogue. Julien continued to greet and engage like this and send consistent signals that he wanted to work together to build a positive culture in the department. The decision to reinitiate those greetings set the positive process in motion.

With time and the consistent effort of all faculty, the department was indeed successful in changing its course and stands today as an exemplary unit of collegiality. But more importantly, Julien and the employee became good friends. They've now worked together on a number of initiatives and projects and have grown to like and respect one another.

The creative power of communication reminds each of us that what we say and do has consequences. The way you communicate in this very moment shows others who you are as a person, what you believe in, and how you want to connect with them. Communication is the very process of relating. It cannot be separated from the world of our relationships with others. If you change the way you communicate, you will change the nature of your relationships.

As we have shown here, positive leaders move in the direction of others. They initiate contact and open up the possibility of connection. They avoid the silent treatment and keep lines of communication open. And when conflicts arise, they move back in. If you think of communication as having constitutive power, you can alter the direction of any interaction and relationship. Then you can take it to the next level by creating the conditions that will enable people across your unit to connect with one another.

LEVEL 3: INVITE DIALOGUE

For leaders, the act of greeting is also the act of inviting others to connect. Part of your responsibility is to foster an environment in which people work well together, connect with one another, and support each other. In this section, we share two main strategies to create consistent opportunities to invite dialogue across your organization.

Strategy 1: Create Space for Mutual Connections

One of the most important strategies you can use is to create lots of opportunities for your people to meet one another and connect more often. There are no limits to how you could approach this. Your motivation to help connect people will make a world of difference.

For three years, Julien served as dean of a college with 1,600 students and 125 faculty and staff. One of his core goals was to bring people together across academic areas to build a real sense of community. To do so, Julien and his team outlined a five-year goal to build community in the college. Every year, the team would decide what initiatives to create, maintain, or lead. But the ideas were simple.

To invite people together, the leadership team created numerous initiatives. For instance, they developed a yearly annual conference at which faculty, staff, students, and alumni from different areas of study presented their work together and celebrated their successes. The team also developed a number of small regular events. For faculty and staff, he organized small monthly "conversation cafés." In a small space for seven to eight people, Julien offered drinks and pastries from a local coffee shop and asked every person to share their journey, the focus of their research, and their passion for teaching. These gatherings were by invitation only, scheduled for 30 to 45 minutes, but always lasted at least 60 minutes because of the meaningful conversations that took place. For students, he developed a monthly lunch with the dean at which students across seven academic disciplines would meet each other. The sole purpose of the meeting was for students from different disciplines to get to know one another, build initial connections, and share lunch. Clearly, food helps connect people!

These events are designed to increase the number of connections and expand the informal network of people who already share connections. If done consistently, their impact is measurable. The more people meet one another, the more they learn about each other. In that process, not only are people creating a sense of community and belonging, but the knowledge they have about each other makes collaborations and friendships more likely. Consider the number of connections Julien made:

- Coffee with faculty/staff (held monthly with 8 individuals): 96 connections per year
- Student coffee with alumni (held biweekly with 10 students): 240 connections per year
- Student lunch with the dean (held monthly with 15 students): 180 connections per year

With these three simple initiatives and a little effort, Julien made a minimum of 516 connections per year between himself and others. This does not include the fact that every person attending also expanded their own networks by meeting each other. Sometimes, inviting connections involves careful planning and implementation, as in these events. At other times, small initial steps create their own momentum. It's up to you as the leader to identify what your people need and find creative ways to meet those needs.

Strategy 2: Identify and Address People's Needs

Leaders must constantly look for ways to encourage connections on their own teams and throughout their organization. Each team has its own unique needs and quirks. Opportunities for connection surround every leader.

We were speaking recently with Kristen Eichhorn, dean of graduate studies at SUNY Oswego. She relayed a story about her efforts as a new departmental supervisor to create an inviting environment to help her faculty connect. She explained, "Our department had gone through a lot of changes. These changes produced anxiety for the faculty, many of whom were working towards tenure. We had four different units that were [historically] functioning separately and there was little appetite for cross-collaborations. During this time of transition and uncertainty, the faculty turned inward. The only thing the faculty knew for sure is that if they shut the door, they could get some of their individual work done. But we're a department of communication. As a new chair, I had to ask myself 'What kind of culture do we want to create?' I knew I had to do something to get these great people out of their offices to connect with each other so they could see the gifts in each other's contributions."

"To start," Kristen continued, "I asked each of them what would make their work environment more comfortable. I discovered people wanted two things. They wanted access to clean drinking water [because the pipes were old] and they often mentioned access to hot coffee. So, I went to the store and bought a Keurig coffee maker. I bought 12 'K cups' and I put them out on the counter in the hallway alcove. Later that week, I came out of my office and I saw two people at the Keurig machine talking, two people who I would not normally see talking. It looked just like the old 'water cooler' conversations we used to have in the workplace. The previous supervisor would have said, 'Good luck with those two.' But here it was playing out right in front of me. They were talking about the coffee flavors. 'What are you drinking?' 'Wild Blueberry.' 'I didn't know they had blueberry.' The next day I heard talking again, 'Guess what I found. Hot chocolate.' Oh, I'll trade you a wild blueberry for a hot chocolate.' I then convinced the faculty to chip in $10 each for the year to bring in a water service. For this small fee, we were able to have access to great water all year. We situated a donated table in the alcove to give people a place to sit. With a coffee maker, water, and a table, we created a physical environment to facilitate those conversations. Faculty started gathering outside of their offices to grade, have lunch, and share stories."

After sharing this story, Kristen shared the lesson that this experience had taught her. She said, "Effective leadership and relationship building is often in the details, the smallest details. Rather simple changes can produce outcomes that can start to change a culture." Whether a leader's plans to invite connection are carefully crafted or emerge almost spontaneously, many followers will simply join in.

You can use the power of positive communication to connect people with one another. You can invite conversation and create spaces for people to interact with both task completion and relationship building in mind. No matter what your role is, the nature of your responsibilities, the number of people you oversee, or your own organizational culture, you have the opportunity to create moments of connection and to foster that in the world of others. The only limit is your own creativity.

When you create moments of connection,
you foster a culture of high-quality relationships.

LEVEL 4: PUT IT INTO PRACTICE

Individually, the small behaviors and decisions we've discussed can have an immediate impact. Collectively, they can begin to change the long-term quality of the relationships in your life and on your team. Let's distill some concrete practices you can use to communicate more positively. Circle the takeaways in the following that would help you the most.

Level 1: The Power of Greetings

- **Initiate greetings and build relationships.** The first step in the right direction is to initiate regular contact with your supervisor, peers, and anybody you supervise. If you are working face to face, initiating contact may be as simple as briefly stopping by the offices of people around you each day to say "Good morning. How was your weekend?" Make a habit of taking the long route on your way back from the restroom or printer to connect with more people.
- **Make time for greetings and connection.** Leave extra time to allow for personal connection. Schedule space on your calendar between meetings to avoid rushing people out the door. Instead of sending emails, get out of your office and meet with others in person on their turf, especially anybody you supervise. You might even schedule several hours per week to simply roam the workplace and touch base with people.
- **Open interactions with care and attention.** The openings and closings of conversations set the tone. Greet people with warmth, care, and an extra dose of old-fashioned etiquette. This positive attention might include genuine politeness and appreciation, direct eye contact, a smile, and perhaps a handshake.
- **Start and finish your emails thoughtfully.** Take an extra moment to make sure you are opening and closing your emails and other written messages well. If done sincerely, this is not only classy, it also creates a more positive atmosphere.

Level 2: Create Meaningful Relationships

- **Create a network of connections.** Communication is the process that creates your relationships at work. Start new relationships and cultivate existing ones.
- **Avoid the silent treatment.** We see the act of greeting others well primarily as the leaders' responsibility. Don't allow your people to feel isolated or ignored. Never use "the silent treatment" to handle difficulties. When you see others in the hallway or walk into a room, be sure to initiate a greeting. This is true for both one-on-one and group situations.
- **Take the initiative to restart the connection.** Inevitably, we've all experienced friction with our supervisors, peers, and direct reports along the way. When this happens, temporary space might help. Still, it's up to the leader to take the brave step to thoughtfully reinitiate contact and affirm professional relationships before too much time has passed.

Level 3: Invite Dialogue

- **Increase the number and frequency of connections.** Schedule meaningful events and establish other occasions to invite people to connect. These could be purely social events or involve some task-related activities. Consider providing food to create a more social atmosphere.
- **Identify and address people's needs.** Keep your eyes open for the need-specific opportunities your team has. What types of time, space, or resources do they need to make their own connections? Look for ways to create the ideal conditions for people to connect on their own.

CONCLUSION

James Humes wrote that "the art of communication is the language of leadership."[17] In this chapter, you have learned the first principle for mastering that language: **when you greet, you create human connection.** We encourage you to make high-quality greetings a daily priority. As a leader, you can make a habit of choosing to greet others, welcoming interaction, and creating lots of little moments for connections. You can proactively reengage with people in spite of conflicts or tension. You can be the driving force to put practices in place that will get people connected. All of these choices will help you develop a positive workplace environment and a community of belonging for your stakeholders. And no matter how busy you are, no matter how serious your workplace, there's always time to initiate connection, as the following example shows.

In 1989, United Flight 232 was scheduled to fly from Denver to Chicago.[18] About an hour into the flight, an explosion in the rear-mounted engine rocked the jumbo jet. Debris from the exposure sliced through the tail section of the plane, including the lines in the hydraulic system that controlled the plane's elevation and steering. This left the captain, Al Hayes, and first officer, Bill Records, unable to steer the plane. In most cases like this, no one survives.

Still, as the crew wrestled for control over the plane, an off-duty pilot, Danny Fitch, left his passenger seat in the cabin, approached the cockpit, and offered to help. Together, the pilot, copilot, and Danny Fitch worked together and used a novel approach to roughly steer the plane by adjusting the thrust in the engines, a job that took all three of them. They somehow managed to crash land the jet at an airport in Sioux City, Iowa, resulting in a massive fire. Out of 296 passengers, 184 survived and 112 people died, many from smoke inhalation that followed the crash. Captain Al Hayes was later praised for his life-saving leadership.

There is a crucial detail in this story that many writers miss. When Danny Fitch, the off-duty pilot, approached the cockpit and offered to help, the pilot, Al Hayes, did what researchers saw as a "remarkable act given the unfolding crisis," which immediately communicated the values of calmness and respect: "Captain Haynes stopped what he was doing, turned around, and shook his [Danny Fitch's] hand." The teamwork in the cockpit that followed was no coincidence. It was the outcome of good leadership. You can do that too by choosing what you implement from this chapter (see box 2.6).

Positive leaders greet to invite a human connection.

Box 2.6. **Top Takeaways**

Reflecting on your selections in the "Level 4: Put It into Practice" section, what are your top three takeaways?

1.

2.

3.

3

Ask to Discover the Unknown

John Maxwell wrote: "Good leaders ask great questions that inspire others to dream more, think more, learn more, do more, and become more."[1] One thoughtful question is all it can take to create deep change.

Tererai Trent is from Zimbabwe, a small nation in the southern region of Africa. By the time she was 17, she was married and raising three young children in her village. Growing up and living in desolation and poverty, Tererai was not sent to school or encouraged to pursue an education, but she learned to read and write by studying from her brother's books. In a chance encounter, she met Jo Luck, an up-and-coming executive at Heifer International, a global nonprofit whose "mission is to end hunger and poverty while caring for the Earth." That meeting changed her life forever.

In 1991, Jo Luck visited her village to explore possibilities for partnerships with Heifer. Sitting together in a circle with a dozen women from the same village who were living in total poverty, Jo talked to them about Heifer and asked for their input and thoughts. At some point in the conversation, Jo saw that Tererai had not spoken yet, so she asked her directly, "You've been quiet. What are your dreams? What are your hopes?" Tererai was scared to speak up in front of the others. She took a moment to pause but knew instantly what she wanted to do. "I want to have an education. I want to have an undergraduate degree, a master's degree, and a Ph.D." "I don't know how I got the courage to share my dreams," Tererai said in a TEDx talk delivered a few decades later. Jo told her, "If you believe in your dreams, they are achievable."[2]

Tererai ran to her mother and told her what had happened. "If you believe in what this woman has said to you and you desire these dreams and you work hard to achieve these dreams, not only are you defining who you are, but you are also defining every life that comes out of your womb for generations to come." "Tinogona," she told her in her native language, "it is achievable." Then, her mother told her to write down her dreams on a piece of paper and to bury them in the ground.

Tererai then worked on her dreams. She took eight years to study and earn her GED. "Eight years of abuse," she explained, "Eight years of struggling to get the next tuition for the next class that I needed to correspond, but eight years of never giving up." After completing her degree, she was accepted as an international student at Oklahoma State University, where she earned bachelor's and master's degrees. Twenty years after she had buried her dreams in the soil of her village, she completed her doctorate in social work.

Tererai then remembered what her mother had said: she needed to not just think of herself, but also give back to her community. Supported by a generous gift from Oprah Winfrey, she founded a school for girls in her home country and began to give back.

Tererai's life story offers lots of lessons. But there is one that aligns especially well with the focus of this chapter. As a leader, Jo Luck was able to use the power of questions to inspire Tererai to pursue her dreams. "What is your dream?" she asked, "What are your hopes?" As questions often do, they set in motion a sequence of events that can alter not just the nature of our immediate interactions, but more importantly the shape and course of our lives. For her part, Jo Luck was promoted to president and CEO of Heifer International several years after this fateful conversation.

In this chapter, you'll learn the second fundamental principle of positive communication: **ask (open-ended) questions to discover the unknown.** Merely telling people what to do or "talking at" them can sometimes be a motivating stimulus for a response. But asking questions is often a much more powerful way to lead others. In this chapter, you will learn to ask better questions. You'll learn the types of questions that open interaction rather than close it. Then you'll learn how to hijack your automatic response system and place yourself in a position of discovery. Finally, you'll level up your skills to harness the power of questions to lead organizational change.

Peter Drucker once wrote: "The leader of the past was a person who knew how to tell. The leader of the future will be a person who knows how to ask."[3] In that spirit, this chapter shows you how to be a leader of the future.

LEVEL 1: THE POWER OF QUESTIONS

This section illustrates how what you say in a conversation shapes the other person's response. We make a fundamental distinction between two types of questions: one that will limit your conversations with your team and one that will expand what is possible. This section is about learning to make that shift as a leader. But to do so, you will first need to change your mindset and then learn to ask new and more positive questions.

Questions set in motion a sequence of events that can alter not only the nature of our immediate interactions, but more importantly the shape and course of our lives.

Habit 1: Shape What Happens Next

In the early 1960s, famed sociologist Harvey Sacks worked at a suicide counseling hotline in Los Angeles.[4] The call center was designed to offer support for people who needed someone to talk to. They asked Sacks to find out why callers were reluctant to reveal their names. Sacks started the painstaking process of transcribing the call center's audio-recorded calls to look for potential solutions. What he found instead changed the fields of linguistics, sociology, and communication.

As he explored the transcripts, he saw that language was organized by turns of talk and that each turn of talk—for instance, whatever the hotline counselors said or asked—projected what the caller might say next. What one person says, he learned, has a direct impact on what the other person says. This is especially visible when somebody asks a question. Here is a simple example:

Person A: Do you prefer the color blue or the color yellow?

Person B: Yellow.

First, Sacks found that people organize virtually all their conversations like this. One person says something, then another person responds. I talk, you talk, I talk, you talk.

Second, he found that how a question is asked will shape what the next person can reasonably talk about. If a question is about a person's color preferences, the next response will be related to colors in some way. The topic is being shaped by the question itself. Third, as seen earlier, some questions reduce all possible responses to only a few choices (in our case, "yellow" or "blue").

Questions then influence the territory of possible responses. They constrain or open up conversations. Even though questions lead to what most people actually talk about, few use their power. Think about it this way: only 6 percent of all acts of communication are questions. However, 60 percent of what we say is in response to questions.[5]

The power of questions comes from the fact that they shape the next turn of talk. Questions focus our attention and lead how others will respond.

Researchers in the field of neuroscience have shown, for instance, that when somebody asks us a question (e.g., What kind of car do you drive?), our brains will pause and become immediately preoccupied until we supply an answer. Questions can be extremely motivating, too. A classic study by a team of researchers showed that merely asking about participants' intention to purchase a car in the next six months dramatically increased their likelihood to buy a car.

For leaders, mastering the art of asking good questions is especially important. Consider these facts backed by empirical research:

- √ Leaders who ask meaningful questions for input are seen by others as increasing effectiveness.[6]
- √ Leaders who ask meaningful and respectful questions create more encouraging work relationships.[7]
- √ Individuals who ask questions and listen deeply are more likely to be perceived as leaders.[8]
- √ Leaders who ask good questions successfully motivate their employees.

In a recent summary of research on the power of questions for leaders, Professor Niels Van Quaquebeke explained that employees feel valued when leaders ask them good questions. "You feel," he said, "that someone cares, that you are competent, and you feel autonomy, that you have some degree of control."[9]

But not all questions are created equal. That's another thing Harvey Sacks discovered: the way you ask the question significantly shapes what comes next.

Today, researchers make a crucial distinction between two types of questions. Some questions are closed-ended. They are designed to limit and constrain what people can talk about. Other questions are open-ended. They liberate the interaction and give people the freedom to choose what to reveal and what not to reveal.

Many people, especially leaders who are on the go and put out fires all day, are drawn to using closed-ended questions. They are like lawyers in a courtroom.

"Have you been able to reach our clients?"

"Can you please cancel my 4 o'clock meeting?"

"Did you go to the conference?"

Although these questions may be helpful to get information, they are ineffective at building and maintaining relationships and constrain the process of discovery. That's because closed-ended questions *limit* the answers one may give in return and are often answered with just one word.[10]

Here is what is likely to happen with the three preceding questions:

Question: Have you been able to reach our clients?
Response: Yes.
Question: Can you please cancel my 4 o'clock meeting?
Response: No problem.
Question: Did you go to the conference?
Response: Yup.

Questions like these can be useful in some circumstances, but they too often limit, constrain, and control what the interaction is all about. And if most of your interactions follow this script, you are not giving others the opportunity to elaborate, explain, or become fully engaged. When you use closed-ended questions, you are making conversations feel mechanical and controlling. You are also short-circuiting the possibility of more meaningful conversations. In fact, if you feel as though your conversations tend to reach a "dead end," you may be either (a) not asking enough questions to create momentum or (b) asking too many closed-ended questions. So, you need to change the questions you ask.

Habit 2: Ask Open-Ended Questions

Positive leaders make a paradigm shift by asking open-ended questions. Open-ended questions are more effective because they are designed to give the next speaker the freedom to choose how much to reveal and what to say. The keyword here is "freedom," the opportunity to choose what to reveal and what not to reveal. Consider a few examples:

- What did you do this weekend?
- How is your project coming together?
- What do you like to do for fun?

Questions like these give the other person more latitude to express themselves. They do not force the person to disclose but simply invite more meaningful communication. Most people we've talked to say that when people ask open-ended questions, the climate in the relationship is "interesting," "personal," "human," and "more vulnerable," and it creates the desire to ask even more questions because now people are in a position to discover.

Open-ended questions are indispensable tools to spark an authentic back-and-forth, collaborative exchange. Open-ended questions typically start with words like "how," "what," or "why." It's difficult to answer questions like this with one-word answers. A single open-ended question like, "What do you think?" can lead to a great discussion with deep engagement. Open-ended questions also signal a mutual respect between leaders and followers. When a leader asks questions such as "What is your opinion?" or "How do you feel about X?," that puts the leader in a place of discovery and empowers others to shape their context.

"Positive questions," researchers Niels Van Quaquebeke and Will Felps explained, "are more likely to yield positive results."[11] There are lots of good questions that leaders can draw on depending on the circumstances. For example, if you want to get your employees tapping into their strengths, Van Quaquebeke recommended asking:

- When did you feel truly energized and engaged at work?
- What do you think were the conditions that led to that moment?
- What can you do in the next year to have more of those moments?

Or, if you are engaged in a problem-solving conversation, you might ask questions like these:

- Why are we doing this?
- What has to be done?
- What do you see as the next steps?

These questions should become a habit so you can open up the interaction rather than close it. See box 3.1 to evaluate your question-asking skills in emails.

Box 3.1. **Do You Ask Questions in Emails?**

Instructions: Take a moment to reflect on the types of questions that you ask in your own interactions with others. Open and examine the last three emails you sent at work. Put a check mark next to any communication habits you can confidently say you practiced in those emails.

- ☐ I asked at least one question.
- ☐ I asked at least one open-ended question.
- ☐ I asked more open-ended questions than closed-ended questions.

What do your answers reveal about your tendency to ask questions? How could you improve your question-asking habits to cultivate a mindset of discovery? Would your answers differ if you examined your last three one-on-one conversations?

Habit 3: Use Questions to Build Relationships

Questions create more productive conversations than making statements. Arvind Singhal is a respected professor, speaker, and author. Singhal often tells the story of Dr. Robert Lindberg, a primary care physician who has been listed in "Best Doctors in America" for many years and has a thriving practice.[12] Singhal had the opportunity to shadow Dr. Lindberg at work to learn firsthand how he built a reputation for running his office and engaging with patients effectively.

Instead of directing the interaction in the examination room along the typical predetermined talking points about symptoms, causes, and treatments, Dr. Lindberg focuses instead on patient's stories and listens empathetically. He takes interaction with his patients seriously because it improves their treatment. He said, "I am no longer just the doctor with prescriptions; I strive to be the doctor with relationships."

Dr. Lindberg interacts with patients through a combination of prompts, questions, stories, and self-disclosure to suit the situation. He may notice that a patient looks concerned and inquire, "You look worried," as Lindberg said to a new patient when Arvind Signal was shadowing him. The patient then told Dr. Lindberg about some health-related concerns as well as numerous professional anxieties that were on her mind. Lindberg followed her lead by asking, "What are you doing to take care of yourself?" The conversation gained momentum and opened up. By the end of the appointment, the patient had had the opportunity to be fully heard and reported already feeling relieved—which is a therapeutic experience in its own right—and then received excellent follow-up medical care.

Dr. Lindberg didn't always use this approach. About eight years before meeting Singhal, Dr. Lindberg's office was managed in a mechanical, top-down, and by-the-book fashion. The office had a thick employee manual, countless policies, and a hard-driven office manager. Dr. Lindberg looked at the workplace he had created and decided that his own office was simply "not a nice place to be." Employee turnover was high, and the morale of the remaining employees was low. That motivated him to literally throw out the manual and revamp the office's culture. Dr. Lindberg and his staff now enjoy "more free-flowing conversations . . . [more] trust and mutual respect, [and virtually no] employee turnover." The medical office is financially healthy, and employees report that they "love coming to work" now.

Dr. Lindberg follows several simple but effective guidelines during his interactions with patients. He listens carefully to patients' stories and remembers the details. He "consciously opens conversations with patients, as opposed to closing them with an opinion, a judgment, or a prescription."

A major part of keeping conversations open is by consistently asking questions such as "What else is on your mind?" and then allowing the patient the time and space to say more. Not surprisingly, this often leads to hearing helpful information that patients may have been less likely to talk about had he handled the conversation in a more traditional doctor-patient interaction. In previous years, Dr. Lindberg had relied on a traditional approach that was "interrogative," steered the conversation in a predictable direction, and "cut off the patient if they go off into a tangent." In contrast, he now uses a conversational approach that aims for "a free exchange of ideas." On the face of it, his approach sounds like it could lead to meandering and unhelpful conversations. He has found that the exact opposite is true. His open-ended approach typically "leads to more rapid resolution of what is really at the bottom of that visit, the real reason they are here." When he asks the right questions, patients often tell him exactly what he needs to know and "cut to the chase more quickly."

"Respectful inquiry," Van Quaquebeke explained, "demands a certain level of humility on the part of the boss. Today's managers must admit that they no longer know everything."[13] To communicate more positively, then, learning to draw on the power of open-ended questions is key. In the next section we show you how to make the change in your leadership approach by intentionally placing yourself in a position of discovery.

LEVEL 2: PLACE YOURSELF IN A POSITION OF DISCOVERY

It's up to leaders to position themselves to ask questions and discover what people have to say. Stan Deetz is a world-renowned organizational consultant and professor emeritus of communication studies at the University of Colorado at Boulder.

Stan often relays a story about the way his supervisor inadvertently placed himself in a position for discovery. He explained, "Many places exist where informal, back channel, and around-the-hierarchy conversations can occur. These include kids being on the same soccer team, knowing where a manager gets an after-work drink, an outdoor smoking lounge, shared hobby, and numerous other possible unofficial avenues through which we might connect. One example I personally experienced," Stan explained, "occurred when my dean would regularly visit the men's room on our floor at around the same time of day on the same day of the week. I was stopping in right before my next class, and he was likely stopping in before a regularly scheduled weekly meeting. The first time it happened, he politely asked me, 'How are things going?' Bathroom conversations can feel awkward, but I communicated a few of our departmental highlights and struggles. He offered to help with a difficult situation we were facing. The spontaneous exchange took only a minute but was extremely helpful."

"The following week," Stan explained, "I deliberately showed up at the same time and place to see what would happen. I arrived in the men's room a minute before I anticipated he would, waited, and did a little pretending. When he arrived, he again asked me how things were going. Another brief and helpful conversation followed. I showed up like this every week after that and this pattern continued for the rest of the semester. I don't think he ever caught on that I was not there to use the restroom. Then again, maybe he did catch on and saw the mutual benefit of the conversations and so just kept showing up." Stan and his supervisor accomplished much more while standing in the bathroom than they might have in a formal meeting. The bathroom is obviously not the most practical or inclusive place to meet. Still, our point is about being alert to and creating opportunities to learn more from others.

It's up to leaders to position themselves to ask questions and discover what people have to say.

For leaders, the intention of this chapter is to do what Stan Deetz and his supervisors were doing: put yourself in a position to gain knowledge and information that you would not learn otherwise. In this section we share four critical leadership goals you can accomplish with the power of questions.

Leadership Goal 1: Increase Your Understanding of Others

The most basic function of changing the way you are asking questions is to put yourself in a posture and mindset to discover more about others. This will help you understand people's perspectives, experiences, values, and ways of thinking, all knowledge that will make you a much more effective and empathetic leader. Let's explore a quick scenario.

Imagine that it's Monday morning and you are coming to work. If it's anything like our experience, we all fall back on our routines. As usual, you're walking through the hallway to your desk. As you walk by, you might peek into people's offices, offer a quick "Hello," and ask mechanically, "Did you have a good weekend?" You might hear some routine answers, "Good. How about you?" You then press forward because you want to get to your office to focus on your tasks as soon as possible. Microconversations like this have their place, but they don't do much to help you understand others more deeply.

Now, imagine a simple shift in the way you ask questions. Instead of just glancing in as you walk by, you make a full stop and ask: "Good morning, how are you, John?" You say it with a genuine smile and wait for a response. You then ask: "How did you spend your weekend?" You've asked two open-ended questions, and you're signaling that you are ready to listen. John sees that you are genuinely interested and briefly shares that one of his children has been ill and they spent a good part of the weekend in the emergency room. He explains that his child has been dealing with a lingering virus and they still don't have a specific diagnosis for it. Some recent changes in John's behavior at work are now beginning to make sense. He's seemed preoccupied and down lately. Now you know why. You take a moment to empathize. Asking real questions leads to giving, discovering, and learning.

To be a positive leader, we encourage you to develop a question toolkit that you can use to open conversations, encourage the other person to share, and place yourself in a position of discovery. For example, you might ask questions like these:

- Tell me your story.
- What are some of your personal and professional goals?
- Who are your role models?
- What do you need to thrive as a professional?

Similarly, John Maxwell suggests sample questions that you can draw on to discover more about others.[14]

- What are you learning now?
- What should I read?
- What is the greatest thing you have ever learned in life?

- How has failure shaped your life?
- What have you done that I should do?
- How can I add value to you?

Notice that all these questions invite the other person to share more deeply. Elon Musk, CEO of Tesla, regularly asks job applicants, "Tell me the story *of* your life."[15] It doesn't get more open-ended than that! These questions are designed by their very nature to set up a conversation in which you are discovering more about the other person.

Asking good questions in everyday interactions is like conducting a moment-to-moment audience analysis. What people share will give you lots of insights, data, and perspectives that you can use to make informed leadership decisions. This information can help you find better ways to mentor your staff, provide appropriate feedback, or offer professional development opportunities. It gives you a sense of people's strengths, their hopes, and their realities—all of which you can now respond to in one way or another. This everyday audience analysis will take a pulse of your context and help you prepare your next moves. A question such as What are your thoughts on this? is easy to ask. The answers to such questions are the payoff. Positive questions lead to positive results.

Unfortunately, many leaders never ask questions in the first place because they assume they know the answers. In 2009, for example, PepsiCo hired an outside consulting firm to redesign its Tropicana juice logo and product packaging. It's now considered one of the worst rebrands in marketing history. By all accounts, PepsiCo hired some of the most successful marketing people in the business for the job. Why, then, did the campaign fail?

In the past, Tropicana's logo consisted of a large orange with a drinking straw plunged directly into it. Customers loved the logo, and the package design was instantly recognizable. In contrast, the newly redesigned logo created by the outside marking firm was just a standard-looking glass of orange juice. When Tropicana rolled out its new logo, packaging, and marketing campaign, customers hated it. In comparison to the previous iconic orange-and-straw design, the new one looked comparatively generic and bland. It was so nondescript that existing customers couldn't locate Tropicana juice on the shelves. Sales immediately plummeted.[16]

The campaign failed so completely that PepsiCo switched back to the original design within weeks. The most shocking part of the entire situation was that the outside firm PepsiCo hired to redesign and market the updated logo admitted that they never asked anybody beforehand what they thought of the new logo in either casual conversations or through focus groups. The leaders of the project assumed they knew what their customers and employees would like instead of asking them. In the end, PepsiCo paid the outside firm a remarkable $50 million for the campaign. Those expenses do not include the company's significant loss of sales.

Tropicana provides a cautionary tale. This failure could have been avoided if the marketing firm had asked even a handful of employees or customers one simple question: "This is a new logo we are considering. What do you all think?"

Our point is simple. Use the power of open-ended questions to understand others' views and perspectives more deeply. By doing so, you will equip yourself to meet the basic needs of your team and do your job as a leader even more effectively.

Leadership Goal 2: Give People Voice

Questions also give followers more voice. Employers know employees want to be heard. Studies show that employee voice and empowerment is directly tied to how satisfied they are at work. In fact, "Employees who feel their ideas and suggestions matter are more than twice as likely to report a positive employee experience than those who don't (83 percent vs. 34 percent)."[17] Despite this evidence, many organizations still do little to solicit employees' input.

In 2021, in the heart of the COVID-19 pandemic, many employers faced the "Great Resignation." The *New York Times* reported that 4.5 million people in the United States quit their jobs in November 2021 alone, which is more than twice the average.[18] Although money is sometimes at the heart of changes like this, a significant shift is happening in the workplace. Many workers are seeking new employment because they want to work where they will feel valued and respected. They want to be treated well and empowered. They want a voice. As Eugene Dilan, an international organizational consultant and executive coach, wrote in *Forbes* magazine: "Until now, most businesses have almost exclusively focused on external stakeholders and their bottom line. . . . [employees], too, want to feel valued, respected and included."[19] Employees at all levels from all walks of life want a positive climate in which people can thrive and leaders welcome followers' thoughts, values, experiences, and perspectives. Leaders at all levels of organizations must adapt to these changes and provide consistent opportunities for empowerment and genuine participation.

To meet this new paradigm shift, leaders need to change the way they think about how communication should flow. A few years ago, Alex was conducting 360 interviews as part of a consulting process for an executive at a large entertainment company. The interviews revealed that the leader of this group was incredibly controlling. Her direct reports described her as a chronic micromanager who wanted everybody to do their tasks exactly like she would do them. Essentially, she did the opposite of empowering her employees. She was not allowing them a voice. As a result, her department reported consistently low morale and experienced high turnover.

In one interview, a former direct report put the executive's leadership style in perspective. "Maybe if this were twenty or thirty years ago," the former team member explained, "you could get away with that as an executive. That's probably how she climbed the ladder in the first place. You could micromanage and be a typical 'boss,' but that approach doesn't work anymore. Employees today want to be treated better. They want their supervisors to listen to them and engage them in a more well-rounded way and have the freedom to share their ideas. There's nobody better at making the company money than she is but the company has been clear that bringing in money alone is not good enough anymore. The company has put her on notice about her leadership style, and if she doesn't turn it around then I think she's done."

Employees today want to be treated better.
They want their supervisors to listen to them and engage them
in a more well-rounded way and have the freedom to share their ideas.

This leader could have turned things around and given her employees more input. Sadly, she was unwilling or unable to change her approach and didn't last much longer at the company.

Another executive from a different organization heard similar initial feedback but was willing to try something new. Hollie Packman has been coaching high-level corporate executives for decades. She has seen firsthand how asking questions can play a pivotal role in leaders' development. In a conversation with us, Hollie relayed a recent success story. "I was coaching a Chief Operations Officer (COO) at a fast-growing and industry-leading company with 7,000 employees. The executive I was coaching was a strong, smart leader, but he had a very directive style. He was tempted to 'overly guide' people, you might say. He was 'the answer guy.' He always had the answer when problems came up. During my first coaching session with him, we were beginning to talk about his leadership feedback over lunch. The server came to take our order. The COO explained to the server how he wanted his pasta prepared in extensive detail. He gave a lot of information, the way it should be cooked, flavored, and spiced. When the server walked away, the COO leaned in and said to me, 'I would cook that pasta myself if they would let me go back to the kitchen.'" His interaction with the server mirrored his leadership approach with his team.

Hollie continued, "We laughed and turned our attention to his written 360-feedback report. It showed, on the upside, that the people around him 'love him and see him as insanely smart, highly competent, and high in his leadership capacity.' On the side of development, they saw him as 'harsh, defensive, closed, confusing, that his team is grossly under-developed.' The big-picture approach the COO took was that of an 'on-the-field coach.'" The COO was involved in every aspect of the work and called every shot.

Hollie explained "He was out there on the field with his team during the game. He had a mindset of 'nobody does it better than me.' He is truly good at doing the work, better than anyone on his team. But that was also the reason that his team members were not developing to their full potential. The main change he made [to] turn his leadership approach around was to become an 'off-the-field coach.'"

"Instead of directing his people," Hollie shared, "he started leading through open-ended questions. His new approach became, 'Here's the outcome I want. What do you think? How can we get there?' He asked questions and began listening to his team as if they were the experts, not him. He stopped double-checking them and allowed them the time to fail, learn, and grow. He was blown away by how well the team started to thrive and grow professionally. He benefited too. He became a radically transformed leader, took his first vacation in years, and didn't bring his laptop or work phone."

When leaders adopt an "off-the-field" approach, they look for ways to give their people a voice and help them step up their influence. This can often be accomplished much more easily than we realize. Recently when Alex was the chair of his department, he had an unexpected turning-point conversation with a relatively new faculty member, Veronica. Alex noticed that she was consistently competent and on top of her teaching and research. Sensing she had more to offer, Alex asked a simple question in a one-on-one supervisory conversation, "What else would you like to be involved in around the department?" She responded with enthusiasm and identified two key areas, increasing the department's efforts to recruit new students and developing the internship program. Both had been listed as the department's "areas of needed improvement" for several years. The problem was, nobody had yet demonstrated the will or the skill to make an impact.

When leaders adopt an "off-the-field" approach, they look for ways to give their people a voice and help them step up their influence.

Within weeks of this conversation and solely because of Veronica's efforts, the department was gaining more new majors than usual as she completely revamped the internship process in ways that piqued students' interest. Veronica had a previously unknown talent for creating professional-level graphics, posters, and social media posts. Just as important, she genuinely enjoyed doing these tasks. The quality of the content in her recruiting emails to students was equally engaging, persuasive, and effective. Her work was so good that it instantly raised her personal profile elsewhere on campus, as other faculty and staff noticed how good the department's new approach was and began asking who they had hired to handle the marketing materials. They'd reply, "Oh, Veronica does all of that. You should see what else she can do!" In this case, a question as ordinary as "What else would you like to be involved in around the department?" provided all the space needed for more voice and empowerment.

Leadership Goal 3: Open Up Your Group Meetings

Group meetings offer lots of practical opportunities to ask more questions. Data in this area suggests that over 55 million meetings are held each week. Middle managers spend about 35 percent of their time being part of group interactions, whereas upper management leaders spend over 50 percent of their time in meetings.[20] Like them or not, group meetings are a persistent part of the daily working lives of leaders. Leading with questions creates an environment in which people can learn from each other. Think of good open-ended questions as a green light. You're cueing your team: "I want to hear from you. The floor is yours!" What questions can you ask that will help you accomplish this goal?

A recent experience helps illustrate how this can be done even in remote meetings. Julien was dialing in to another Zoom meeting with the faculty in the department. Once everyone was present, the chair of the department, April, said: "I'd like to start the meeting in a new way. I'd like each of you to think for a moment about all your experiences this month. What has given you the most meaning this month? What experiences at home or at work have given you the most joy?" She added, "You can share whatever makes you feel comfortable. It can be personal or at work, but we would love to hear from each of you."

There was a bit of a pause for a moment. Just imagine lots of introverted professors trying to figure out what to share. Then one faculty member told a story about how proud she was of one of her children and the decisions they were making. She also shared the difficulties of being a parent, which almost everyone around the table could feel as a common experience. Another person disclosed a positive comment that a student had made in the classroom. As the group went from one shared experience to another, empathy, joy, and mutual engagement increased right there in the moment. They each became more relaxed. They laughed together and connected briefly. April's question changed the dynamics of the group. It shaped what we talked about and how we talked about it, all of which created a moment of cohesiveness in the group. See box 3.2 for tips on asking probing questions in groups.

Leadership Goal 4: Manage Conflict and Difficult Conversations

One unavoidable outcome of making discussions more open is disagreement. When people speak up, some friction is inevitable and even necessary. Every workplace has its own set of hot topics that might divide people. If you let them, disagreements can escalate into toxic conflicts. That's why some leaders avoid those discussions altogether. Instead, we recommend anticipating that difficult conversations can and will happen and committing ahead of time to finding a way to work through them together.

Joseph Grenny and his colleagues offered a useful approach in their popular book, *Crucial Conversations*.[21] Curiosity, they explained, "comes from

Box 3.2. Open Up Discussions with Probing Questions

Leaders can open up discussion even further by asking probing questions that spark creativity and problem solving. For example, in his book *The Culture Code*, Daniel Coyle recommends asking questions like the following when the group faces a difficult decision with alternatives on the table:[1]

- "Now, let's see if someone can poke holes in this."
- "Tell me what's wrong with this idea."
- "Anybody have any ideas?"

Questions like these demonstrate that the leader really does want to open the discussion for maximum participation.

Note

1. Coyle, D. (2018). *The culture code: The secrets of highly successful groups.* New York: Bantam.

true humility—a commitment to truth over ego." Leaders, they suggested, can learn to handle difficult conversations by becoming increasingly curious about the other person and using effective questions to dig deeper. The authors suggested three questions that are critical: "How do you see this situation?"; "Tell me more of your thinking on that"; and "What's your view?"

As each of these questions shows, when we become truly curious, the main impulse is to understand. This leadership approach is especially helpful in preventing unnecessary conflicts from emerging. Curious questions like these proactively release potential pressure by expressing people's needs and wants earlier and in productive ways.

This is something Julien experienced firsthand a few years ago when he was working with the department to rebuild a positive culture. The team had already made pretty good progress, but Julien wanted to keep the positive momentum going by getting faculty and staff together in a meaningful retreat. He pitched some of the ideas in meetings, but he kept getting resistance from one of the faculty members. He couldn't put his finger on it, but some of the tension seemed driven by that faculty member's desire to control the situation. During the week after a departmental meeting, she came to see Julien to chat about something. The two sat in his office and made some small talk. Julien then pivoted the conversation by asking her, "You know,

---

Box 3.3. **Move from Blame to Curiosity**

An article by Laura Delizonna in *Harvard Business Review* offers an easy framework to manage difficult conversations.[1] Her process includes three steps to manage any difficult conversation:

Step 1: **Describe the problematic behavior as neutrally as you can.** If your employee is constantly late, you would simply state the following: "I've noticed that you have been late on a consistent basis in the last month."

Step 2: **Show empathy and explore the situation.** "I imagine that there are lots of possible reasons for this. Could we talk together about what's happening?"

Step 3: **Ask open-ended questions to discover solutions together.** You might ask, "Can you tell me more about what's going on with you?" Once you have clarity on the sources of the problem, then you would ask more directly about possible solutions: "What do you think could be done to address this issue?" or "What do you see as possible solutions?"

This effective communication process slows down the interaction, keeps the dialogue open, and helps prevent conversation from turning combative.

Note

1. Delizonna, L. (2017, August 24). High-performing teams need psychological safety: Here's how to create it. *Harvard Business Review*. https://hbr.org/2017/08/high-performing-teams-need-psychological-safety-heres-how-to-create-it

---

we've been talking about hosting a retreat and I was thinking of you and wondered about your thoughts. From your perspective, what would be your ideal for our retreat?" He was genuinely curious. He had no idea how she might answer. Immediately she smiled, and her energy turned positive. She was excited. She said: "I'm really dreaming of a retreat where we can all come together in a meaningful way. I'd love for us to spend some time together, have a chance to eat out as a group, and even spend a few days away from the university so that we can really bond again." She added a few more comments, and Julien listened as deeply as he could.

Once he had heard her dreams and vision, he shared his. He said, "Well, you know everything you've described is exactly what I'm hoping we will accomplish together. We share a similar vision." Julien then described where the retreat would be located, explained what the team would be doing, and ended by asking for her support to make it a successful experience. Her response was immediate: "Of course, I'm happy to help in any way I can." Curiosity-driven communication like this will help you navigate conflicts and other difficult conversations as they emerge. See box 3.3 for more tips on approaching difficult conversations with curiosity.

With these question-asking skills in mind, let's now take you to a whole new level. We focus next on how you can use the power of questions to create a more positive culture in your organization. We will show you how to flip the script of your organizational system to create a culture of belonging and effectiveness.

LEVEL 3: FLIP THE WHOLE SCRIPT

You can apply the power of questions to transform your organizational culture. Two contexts are especially consequential for leaders: performance review and leading organizational change. Here's how questions can help.

Strategy 1: Ask Better Questions in Performance Reviews

A few years ago we visited an organization in Little Rock that had earned several awards for creating a great culture for its employees. We met with Peter, vice president of human resources, to understand what they had done. In the meeting, Peter said, "We used to have a lot of problems. We couldn't retain our employees, morale was at an all-time low, and we even had difficulty hiring people to join our workforce."

"I was at the table when the leadership made the crucial decision to change all that," he added. "We wanted to become known not just for the services we provide, but for our culture and for the ways in which we are doing good for ourselves and for our employees," he explained. "We made our culture the most important thing in this company."

There were lots of things that the leaders started doing differently. They identified their core values, developed a new mission statement, and created a vision for the future. People were even hired and fired based on whether they were contributing to a positive workplace environment. They offered several professional development opportunities, including a popular course on emotional management taught by the vice president of human resources himself. He called it "life changing" because he himself had undergone a dramatic personal transformation from learning about emotional management and a new language to interact with others. It changed who he was as a person, a husband, and a boss, and he wanted all his employees to have a shot at that kind of personal transformation also.

Peter got to the heart of the story: "But there is something important that we did to drastically change our culture; we changed the way we do annual performance evaluations." For a long time the company was doing what most organizations do. It had a yearly evaluation process in which the central task was for the supervisor or manager to assess performance and provide feedback. "We still do a little bit of that," Peter said, "but we've become completely employee centered."

The shift was simple. They asked open and positive questions. Each supervisor and manager would perform evaluations with the purpose of *understanding* their employees' experiences and to build on their strengths rather than their weaknesses. They placed all supervisors in a position to discover their staff and flipped the script on what those conversations happening across the organization were all about. Managers were encouraged to ask questions like these:

√ How can we better serve you this upcoming year?
√ What key strengths would you like to capitalize on this upcoming year?
√ What are some areas that you feel you need more support in to be successful in your role?
√ What professional development opportunities do you need to succeed in your role?
√ What are some areas that you would like to build on and improve?

These questions were the starting point to frame the conversation. Difficult conversations about performance were also encouraged, but those difficult moments were managed in a context in which the employee felt respected all along.

As a leader, you can flip the script of your own interactions. You can also use these moments to learn from employees about areas that you can improve on as a leader. In *The Culture Code: The Secrets of Highly Successful Groups*,

Box 3.4.   **Ask Open Questions in Performance Review Conversations**

Use open-ended questions to promote better performance, mutual respect, and employee growth. Here is a sample we have put together. Put a check mark next to the questions you will incorporate this year.

- ☐ Tell me about your last year.
- ☐ What are some of the highlights for you?
- ☐ What are you most proud of?
- ☐ What do you see as your strengths?
- ☐ What do you see as areas of improvement within your role?
- ☐ What are your hopes for next year?
- ☐ How can we better serve you this upcoming year?
- ☐ What is one thing that I currently do as your supervisor that you'd like me to continue doing?
- ☐ What is one thing that I don't currently do frequently enough as your supervisor that you think I should do more often?
- ☐ What can I do as your supervisor to make you more effective?

Daniel Coyle suggested that you can use a few questions about your own leadership approach to get quick feedback from members of your team. Once again, this should be in a context where relationships have been maintained, but getting feedback from your employees quickly can help you adjust and adapt. Three questions are especially useful:[22]

- √ What is one thing that I currently do that you'd like me to continue doing?
- √ What is one thing that I don't currently do frequently enough that you think I should do more often?
- √ What can I do to make you more effective?

Keep in mind that most professional interviewers and researchers know that the best information often comes at the end of an interview. That's because conversations and relationships take time to warm up. As an interaction unfolds, people begin to feel comfortable with one another and start to disclose information with more freedom and depth. To make improvements to your leadership approach, Julien and Alex recommend ending with a final check with questions like these:

✓ What else would you like to share with me today? It could be anything at all.
✓ Is there anything you've noticed, even something small, that would make a difference?
✓ Is there anything else you would like to mention, no matter how minor or insignificant it might seem? Take a moment to think about it.

See box 3.4 for a distilled checklist of prompts and questions for performance reviews.

Strategy 2: Use Appreciative Inquiry to Lead Change

A second question-driven approach that shifts conversations and ultimately an organization's culture is the process of *appreciative inquiry* (AI). By definition, AI is "a strengths-based, positive approach to leadership development and organizational change."[23] Originally developed by David Cooperrider and Frank Barrett, AI is an approach to conversations designed to get people thinking about strengths, possibilities, and positive solutions on their team rather than dwelling on deficiencies and problems.[24]

AI is especially useful when planning a yearly off-site retreat or other periodic big-picture team gatherings. Many traditional off-site gatherings Julien and Alex have attended, for instance, involve year-end status updates, awards and recognition, and a guest speaker or two. This can be effective in some situations. The better events involve big-picture strategizing and vision casting. Still, in most cases the bulk of the communication, presentations, and "content" at these offsites is merely consumed by relatively passive participants. The most engaging, participative, and memorable off-site events we've seen are driven by an appreciative inquiry approach that is based on the fundamental statement that "a question is only as good as the answer it evokes."[25] In that light, consider designing an off-site experience around these four key steps.

Step 1: **Discover and remind people of what is already great.** Here you need to ask questions that "seek to uncover and bring out the best

in a person, a situation, or an organization."[26] You can easily do this by posing these questions:
- ✓ What do we do well?
- ✓ What are we successful at?
- ✓ What do you value the most about the work that we are doing together as a team?

Step 2:   **Get people to dream big.** Dreaming is simply considering what might be. It can be answered by asking these big questions:
- ✓ What are we dreaming about for ourselves and our work?
- ✓ If we had a magic wand, what workplace environment would we want to create together?
- ✓ Where would we like to be three years from now?

Step 3:   **Help your team imagine what "should be."** At this stage, you are trying to get people thinking more concretely about how to bring to life what they are dreaming about. This can be simply triggered by asking big open-ended questions that might include the following:
- ✓ What are some key practices that we should maintain moving forward?
- ✓ What are specific initiatives and goals that should drive us for the next two to three years?
- ✓ What core values should ground our decisions and behaviors?

Step 4:   **Shape the team's destiny.** At this stage, questions will guide your team to think concretely about the next steps to turn dreams and ideals into action. To do so, you would ask questions like these:
- ✓ What steps do we need to take now to bring our vision to fruition?
- ✓ What are two or three goals that we need to work on immediately?
- ✓ What will each of us do to play our part?

The AI process provides leaders with a conversational plan for creating change. It harnesses the power of purposeful questions to drive creativity and innovative conversations and helps translate those conversations into real-world decisions and action steps. Now that you have learned the power of questions, ways to achieve healthy goals, and how to flip the whole script of your organization, let's implement what you have learned.

LEVEL 4: PUT IT INTO PRACTICE

Let's now draw some of these threads together to make these practices more actionable. As leaders, how can we implement these practices to cultivate a context of discovery on a day-to-day basis? Following are some starting places. Circle the items you'd like to put into practice.

Recognize the Power of Questions

- **Ask more questions.** Rather than "talking at" people, the best starting place to discover is to ask more questions. When leaders ask more questions, the dynamic on the team almost automatically elevates.
- **Ask open-ended questions**. Closed-ended questions can serve a purpose as a jumping-off place, but they often limit conversation. Open-ended questions provide a metaphorical blank canvas for the discussion. Questions like these often lead to new ideas and are naturally stimulating.

Place Yourself in a Position to Discover

- **Increase your understanding of others.** Socialize, create opportunities to connect with your team and colleagues, and ask questions to get to know them and understand their needs. Ask them questions like, "What do you like to do for fun? What are some of your personal and professional goals?"
- **Encourage others to speak in their own voices.** Leaders who truly want team members to speak in their own voices must consistently encourage this. One way is to position yourself as an "off-the-field" coach. Ask your team, "What do you think we should do? What do you suggest? How do you think we should solve the problem?"
- **Open up in group meetings**. Especially at the beginning of meetings, ask questions that bypass the traditional approach. Ask questions like, "What experiences at home or at work have given you the most joy? It can be personal or at work, but we would love to hear from each of you."

Opening meetings like this will help puncture traditional conversational bubbles and get people to open up.

- **Manage difficult conversations.** Use curiosity to co-create solutions as conflicts emerge. We should expect that more open communication might reveal disagreements. We recommend that rather than avoiding disagreements, you should approach these conversations with a genuine disposition of curiosity. Questions driven by curiosity keep conversational partners in a mindset of discovery that is much more likely to lead to collaborative solutions.

Flip the Whole Script

- **Ask better questions in performance reviews.** This involves shifting the focus of performance evaluation so the conversation emphasizes followers' strengths. Ask questions like, "What key strengths would you like to capitalize on this upcoming year?" When it comes to making improvements, ask "What are some areas that you would like to build on and improve?" Positioning followers to lead the discussion gives them ownership and agency over their future.
- **Design off-site sessions using an AI approach**. Teams can design off-site sessions as discussions that are driven by questions that focus on the full range of strengths to bring out the team's best. Sessions can include co-created inspirational conversations that imagine an ideal future for both the workplace's culture and its long-term aspirations as an enterprise. Using this approach puts every participant in the meaningful role of enthusiastic co-creator of a team culture.

CONCLUSION

At the opening of this chapter, Tererai Trent's mother told her, "Tinogona. It is achievable." Tererai's big journey began when Jo Luck asked her: "What are you dreaming about? What are your hopes?" She then used those dreams to take action and design her destiny. Questions, as the chapter shows, can unlock the possibilities within us and our relationships with others. The power of questions comes from placing yourself in a position of discovery, in a stance of humility, and in a place of curiosity. When you ask, you discover. And when you discover, you can flip the structure of your interactions and your organization (see box 3.5).

In one of the interviews for this book, Julien and Alex sat down with Pete Tanguay, a fast-paced business entrepreneur and community leader in central Arkansas. He loves asking his team members questions but clarified, "Not every question is a good question. The question itself is what's going to get you the answer."

"So, you have to learn to ask good questions," he continued, "especially if your goal is to ask questions that will get you an answer you've never thought of. [For that] you've got to learn to ask big mind-stretching questions."

One question Pete really likes to ask to get people to dream big came from someone he listened to on a cassette tape many years ago. The question was this: "What's your 500-year plan?"

"If you think about that for a moment," he said as he took the role of a disbelieving listener, "your first response is to think, 'This is a stupid question. Who's got a 500-year plan? Who can impact the world 500 years from now?'" "Well," he added, "there *are* people who have!" Tererai Trent comes to mind. She changed her life and the lives of her family, and she later created a school in Zimbabwe that will change the lives of hundreds of girls for generations to come. A good question helped make that possible. Using box 3.5, make your own plan for how to incorporate what you learned in this chapter into your leadership style.

Positive leaders ask to discover.

Box 3.5. **Top Takeaways**

Reflecting on your selection in the "Level 4: Put It Into Practice" section, what are your top three takeaways?

1.

2.

3.

4

Compliment to Affect People's Sense of Self

Successful leadership is all about building and maintaining relationships. It involves creating an environment in which people feel valued, respected, and engaged. That in itself is its own reward. Even better, great workplace cultures also enhance employees' and organizational performance. As Herb Kelleher, the founder and chairman emeritus of Southwest, once explained: "You put your employees first, and if you take care of them, then they will take good care of you, and then your customers will come back, and your shareholders will like that, so it's really a unity."[1] This chapter focuses on how you can take care of your employees by expressing, focusing, and building on their strengths.

Consider the following facts:[2]

- Positive employee experience improves job performance.
- The most compelling driver of an employee's performance is the *quality* of the relationship they have with their immediate supervisor.
- Employee recognition preserves and builds the identity of individuals, gives employees meaning, promotes their development, and contributes to their health and well-being.
- Companies with the most effective employee communication programs provided a 91 percent total return to shareholders.
- Employees consider recognition for a job well done, respectful treatment, and coaching and feedback more important than pay.

- Twenty-five percent of HR executives report that a lack of recognition was the most likely factor causing good employees to quit their jobs.
- Unfortunately, less than one in every five workers is actively engaged in their work.

These facts are just the tip of the iceberg but provide a clear direction for how leaders need to communicate with their team. In this chapter you'll learn the third part of the positive communication model: **compliment others to affect their personal growth.** This principle echoes the fundamental belief that communication affects who people are in the moment and who they become in the long run. Complimenting is the purest way to offer positive feedback and tell others the strengths and potential we see in them. It's something you can do at the personal level with others, and it's a tangible strategy to integrate across your organization.

This chapter proceeds as follows. First, you'll learn how and why complimenting is so important in the workplace, why it's sometimes difficult to do, and why many leaders take it for granted. Second, you'll learn to affect your professional relationships with positive communication and strengthen them for long-term success. Third, you will level up the power of compliments to engage your employees on a wider scale.

LEVEL 1: THE POWER OF COMPLIMENTS

A crucial part of leading effectively is delivering genuine, intentional, and meaningful compliments. The spoken word can have a tremendous impact on others. Leaders are positioned to make the most of it. In this section we illustrate the power of complimenting and encourage you to begin doing it more often and with clearer intentions. We offer four key principles.

Principle 1: Compliments Serve as a Mirror for Others

As a leader, you are a mirror for others. The way you relate to other people not only communicates who you are but also reflects how employees come to view themselves. You are constantly sending messages to each person you lead about their identity and value.

In his book *The Presentation of Self in Everyday Life*, Erving Goffman, a renowned sociologist, used a theatrical metaphor to explain how people present who they are and get other people to see them in a certain light.[3] Every moment in our social world is happening as if it were on a stage where people play various roles. Specifically, Goffman wanted to understand what people accomplish when they present themselves this way. What do they say, and for what purposes? What goals do they achieve in conversations through their actions?

One obvious goal that drives our communication and actions is our desire to shape the way others see us. In some conversations, for instance, we may want to be seen as kind, generous, friendly, or outgoing. We may want to display our work ethic or level of intelligence. For example, have you ever "presented" yourself in a certain way to make a desired impression in a job interview, on a date, or during an important conversation?

Goffman's approach to communication should be especially interesting to leaders. In addition to presenting ourselves to others, we also communicate who we think *they* are to us. When we present ourselves in our role as a leader, parent, or teacher, for example, we simultaneously cast others in the counterpart roles of follower, child, or student. In short, we hold up a mirror with our communication that reflects how we see others.

Take a look at the following interaction between Renae and Kamesha. Notice how each person in the conversation "presents" their role and simultaneously reflects the role and identity of the other person. As you read the conversation, keep these questions in mind:

- Who is the supervisor in this exchange? Who is the direct report? How do you know that?
- What identities is each person presenting about themselves?
- What identities is each person giving the other?

Renae: So, Kamesha I want you to know I consider you to be a strong team player and I just don't know what I would do without you.

Kamesha: Thanks, Renae. That means a lot, especially coming from you. I certainly try my best, and I truly enjoy working for you.

Renae: The thing is, I plan to retire in a few years, and I know that you are in school. I don't see why you wouldn't be a perfect person to take over once I leave.

Kamesha: Wow! I never thought about it, but it does seem like a wonderful opportunity.

Renae: So do you plan to go to graduate school?

Kamesha: Well, to be honest, I really want to go to law school. It's been my lifelong dream. I know it really doesn't tie into this job, but it's my dream.

Renae: Don't be remorseful about following your dream. I think you can do whatever you put your mind to. You are smart and ambitious, and I think you would be a great attorney. Good for you for setting your goals high.

You probably noticed fairly early in the exchange that Renae is the supervisor and Kamesha is the direct report. Their string of mutually complimentary words reflects back like a mirror on the other person. Renae tells Kamesha that she is a strong team player, that she is valuable, and that she could be a great future leader for this organization. She tells Kamesha that she is smart and ambitious. Kamesha values Renae's thoughts, opinions, and ideas as her supervisor.

Even brief conversations like this are packed with implications. People develop a sense of who they are in part based on the way other people talk to them even in everyday conversations like Kamesha and Renae's. As a leader, the extra influence with which you "speak into" the lives of your followers should motivate you to take compliments seriously. Leaders' words literally affect who others are in the moment and shape who they might become.

Your compliments communicate how you see others but also shape profoundly how they see themselves.

Principle 2: Compliments Create Profound Moments of Influence

At the most basic level, your compliments should communicate the strengths you see in others. This can have a profound influence, as Taneshia's experience illustrates.

Taneshia works as an education counselor at a public university. She meets with students every day to help them succeed. "Communicating is so powerful," she said in an interview. "And you want to make sure that you are putting something positive in the world. People remember. People retain."

In her role, she expresses this to students directly. "A lot of students feel like they won't be successful. They are just here to give it a try. And I have to have those conversations with them." She tells them, "You got this. We're here to support you. . . . Watch what you say, even if it's about yourself."

> ## Box 4.1. **A Memorable Compliment**
>
> **Instructions:** Take a moment to reflect about your own experience as an employee:
>
> - What is one compliment that you have received in your professional career that has meant a great deal to you?
> - Who gave you this compliment, and how did it affect you in the short and long term?
> - When you have identified what was said, write it out exactly as it was said to you. Write down the compliment here:

Taneshia now spends her working days reminding students that words are powerful, in part because she also benefited from someone who helped her succeed.

"It was my college night in high school," Taneshia shared. "I was a normal kid, an average student making average grades, and I was an athlete. I didn't really consider [going to] college because my family was so poor, and I didn't have a way to pay for it."

"At our college night, a recruiter asked me, 'What do you want to be when you grow up?' I never really thought about it. My goal was to finish high school successfully," she said. "I wasn't going to get a scholarship."

She told the recruiter, "I don't think I'm college material."

The recruiter stopped her right in her tracks. "You can be anything you want to be. This school is offering you a chance to go to school. You don't know until you try."

Taneshia applied and was soon accepted into the college. Her recruiter stayed with her, too. "He followed me throughout my first two years in college," she explained. "He was a steady voice of encouragement."

When she transferred the recruiter told her, "'Be confident, be strong, and be resilient.' Those words are my foundation. I am probably the most resilient person you've ever met. It is so hard for me to give up on anything that I start, and I have built myself up on his words. They were so strong, so powerful. So, I seriously built my life on those three adjectives."

Taneshia's story captures one of the most important truths of human communication: what we say and do affects people. Our words and actions have consequences and ripple effects on other people's identities, which also reflect back on us.

This may not have been the first time a leader complimented and encouraged Taneshia, but this time the words landed. It all started because the recruiter expressed the strengths and potential he saw. As a leader, you need to find ways of expressing the strengths you see in your team members. When you share compliments, you are creating a profound moment of influence. See box 4.1 to reflect on a memorable compliment.

Principle 3: Meaningful Compliments Make Memorable Moments

Most of us have experienced a moment of communication that has affected us positively. It might be a quick word from a colleague, encouraging feedback from a supervisor, or support provided by a spouse or friend. Messages like these usually stay with us. They become what we call *memorable messages*, which people remember for long periods of time and that have a major influence on their lives.[4] Those moments can be short or even occur in passing. But the message has a way of always sticking because it's what we needed to hear whether we realized it or not. And we can draw positive, encouraging energy from that message right there in the moment and also for years to come. Leaders can and should make the most of this. In fact, more than 50 percent of memorable messages in the workplace come from people employees directly report to or look up to, including their direct supervisor or a significant leader in the organization.[5]

Just as you probably have done, both Julien and Alex have experienced memorable moments with supervisors and leaders in the past. Fresh out of college, Alex's first full-time job was at a human services organization that employed several hundred people. After about a year on the job, he told the team he had decided to go to graduate school. On his last day, Alex's supervisor told him, "Before you leave today, Scott wanted you to visit him upstairs." Scott was the director of the entire organization. He was known as highly competent, perceptive, fair, and kind. Scott welcomed Alex warmly into his office and said, "I heard this was your last week with us and I just wanted to thank you for working here this past year. I've heard nothing but great stuff about you." "Well, thank you for hiring me. I've had an excellent experience here," Alex replied. Scott added, "Over the years, I've seen many people come and go. Most of them work on their teams, and, in the long run, make a real difference in people's lives." He continued, "But, some people have the kind of qualities that help them make that same impact within just five minutes of meeting a person. I see you as one of those people. And I know that whatever you end up doing, you're going to continue to make that difference." In disbelief, Alex asked himself for weeks following this meeting, "Is Scott right? Can I really have that kind of positive impact?" To this day, the compliment remains a standard Alex is striving to live up to. It took him several years to realize that Scott himself was one of those five-minute-impact people. He used the short time he had with Alex solely to build him up, with no expectations of any return on that investment for the organization Alex was leaving.

Similarly, early in Julien's career as a junior faculty member, he was sitting in his office one late Friday afternoon. Out of the blue, the phone rang. "Hi, Julien. This is David Belcher," the voice said. At the time, Dr. David Belcher was provost and chief academic officer, the highest academic position at the University of Arkansas at Little Rock. Dr. Belcher was competent, well-liked, and respected. He was leaving the university to become chancellor at Western Carolina University, where he became one of its most beloved leaders. Julien was struck by the phone call because they had only interacted a few times. After a short greeting, Dr. Belcher said, "As you may know, I'm transitioning to Western Carolina University, and I'm making a few calls around campus to people I really believe in." He added, "I wanted to tell you that you are doing such great work and bringing to the table so many strengths. I can't wait to see the contributions you are going to make to this institution. You are going to be a great leader for the institution in the next ten years." Julien could not believe it. This brief conversation gave him confidence, self-belief, and hope for his career. David Belcher was known for his leadership, but what made him great was what he did in small, less public conversations, like calling faculty and staff individually around campus to intentionally compliment them and share his respect.

Both stories illustrate two leaders who made a significant difference through the act of complimenting. They were thoughtful, meaningful, and memorable compliments that affected us in the moment and over time. Take a moment to reflect on your own habits when it comes to compliments in box 4.2.

The act of complimenting is critical to the way you communicate overall. Most of us look up to our leaders. Their words often carry extra weight when it comes to how we feel about and ultimately see ourselves. That makes it even more important to give meaningful, memorable compliments.

Principle 4: Affirmative Feedback Adds Value: Get Past Your Resistance

Despite the many advantages of complimenting, many leaders do not offer regular compliments, for lots of understandable reasons. Leaders get busy and overwhelmed and may feel that they don't have time. Some people feel

---

Box 4.2.   **Do You Give Compliments?**

Instructions: Think about your own tendency to compliment others. Take a moment to answer these questions:

- To what extent do you make an effort to compliment others?
- How often do you compliment your staff and celebrate their strengths? How often do you criticize them or point out possible improvements they could make?
- When is the last time that you seized an opportunity to express a simple compliment?
- When did you last write a simple note to do so?
- Have you done any of this in the last seven days?

Given your answers, write out some concrete goals you can set for giving more compliments in the coming days.

Notes:

that offering sincere compliments puts them in a vulnerable position. Some people avoid doing so because it can feel awkward. Other people may have an overly competitive spirit and don't want to risk lifting other people up or giving someone a "big head." Sometimes leaders simply do not believe people need or even thrive on positive feedback.

Still, from an objective and big-picture view, the case for giving compliments is difficult to debate. People are desperate for positive feedback. Gallup, Inc., the Washington-based analytics company, has been studying the influence of positive feedback in the workplace for decades. Gallup, for example, "discovered that building employees' strengths is a far more effective approach than a fixation on weaknesses."[6] Research has also shown the following:

√ The "vast majority (67%) of employees who strongly agree that their manager focuses on their strengths or positive characteristics are engaged, compared with 31% of employees who strongly agree that their manager focuses on their weaknesses."[7]

√ Eighty-three percent of employees "who received recognition when doing work" reported having a positive employee experience with their employer.[8]

√ Employees who have a more positive experience are twice as likely to take the initiative to do extra work.[9]

Compliments, recognition, and positive feedback all add obvious value. In light of such compelling data, we challenge you to overcome any personal resistance you might have to giving compliments, positive feedback, or praise. An experience we recently heard from Anne Ricketts shows how leaders' reluctance to give positive feedback can influence a team.

Anne, the executive coach we mentioned in an earlier chapter, shared a story about a director in a Silicon Valley company who was having trouble offering positive feedback about a year into the COVID-19 pandemic. Anne explained, "I was working recently with a director at a technology company. In general, she's nice, warm, and approachable. But the pandemic has been exhausting for leaders. In the middle of it, she discovered that two of her high-performing managers on her team were leaving. She tried to convince them to stay but they basically told her point blank, 'too little too late.' The director had already received feedback in the past that her people needed more positive affirmation, but she never made the adjustment because she personally doesn't need it from her own supervisors. She didn't realize that the absence of positive feedback was an issue for others on her team. She just thought to herself, 'They are working at one of the top tech companies. They already know they are great.'"

"When two of her top managers left," Anne continued, "it made her realize more deeply that the people on her team needed more positive feedback. She talked to a few more people, and it became clear there was a problem. Her employees were wondering, 'Am I valued here? Am I in the right place?'" With the help of Anne as her coach, the director brought the team together and owned up to her mistakes. She told them, "'Yes, these managers have left. Here are my mistakes. How can we move forward together?' She received a good response after the meeting. Her team members were saying, 'This conversation is what I needed.'" Anne explained, "The experience also made her realize that just because she's a leader doesn't mean she has to be stoic."

The director's experience shows us both sides of the story. People crave positive feedback, compliments, and other forms of affirmative recognition, especially from their leaders. When they don't get it, they may very well decide to look for it elsewhere.

In summary, compliments are positive mirrors that reflect how we see others. Compliments express the strengths we see in them and create powerful and memorable moments. They also provide lots of value to followers and to the team. Next, let's level up and strengthen your relationships at work.

LEVEL 2: COMPLIMENTS STRENGTHEN RELATIONSHIPS

In the long run, compliments can be instrumental in strengthening your relationship with others. In a recent interview, we sat down with Julie, a director of organizational development for a large not-for-profit healthcare system. In her role, she helped to build an organization well-known for its focus on patient care, positive culture, and employee support. She is energetic, is enthusiastic, and can juggle a thousand thoughts all at once. She is also supportive and can effectively coordinate a team to maximize its potential.

Julie coaches top leaders in her health-care organization. She said, "The feeling of love, you can't touch it, but you can feel it. You know it's there. You can sense it." She added, "You know when you are around someone who is really loving what they're doing. You just know."

"It goes right back to employee engagement," Julie explained. Some of the executives she coached would be so excited "about someone on their team that had really done a great job." But she also asked them, "'Did you tell them? Did you recognize them in some way? I'm not saying publicly, but in a one-on-one conversation? It's extremely meaningful.'" "I remember one specific conversation when this leader said to me, 'You know, I have told everyone else but probably not them,'" Julie said.

Julie gave us more context. "You know this one employee was just such a rock star and they were starting to have a difficult relationship" and the employee did not feel valued at all. "So, it kind of got down to just one-on-one, have you told them? Like, with your words?," she said with a laugh. "It is so simple," she added, "but it was kind of an 'aha moment' for him." "'I don't know why I haven't done that,'" the leader said to her. Julie then encouraged him: "'Take this person to coffee or even an elevator ride, it takes no time.'"

"Just do it," she exclaimed. And when you do it, she said, "it takes off in your department. It continues to grow. You compliment, and suddenly, someone else compliments. It grows bigger and bigger."

Julie is 100 percent correct. Employee compliments and recognition are key ways of "preserving and building the identity of individuals, giving their work meaning, promoting their development and contributing to their health and well-being."[10] Without positive feedback like this, employees may ask themselves, "What's the point of all of this?" Not surprisingly, studies have shown that the lack of recognition was a common reason good employees quit their jobs.[11] If we take a long-term view, compliments also invest in the other person's future.

As a leader, complimenting not only strengthens your position but also strengthens your relationships with your followers. Think of yourself as a "talent scout" of sorts. By building the habit of giving sincere compliments, you will focus your attention on the very best that people have to offer. If you're looking for the positive qualities in others, you are more likely to see them and engage with others with their positive qualities in mind. In addition, as people experience this sense of positive attention and effort toward them, they will naturally begin to reciprocate. This process then strengthens the long-term, positive bond between leaders and followers for everybody's benefit.

But the crux of the challenge with complimenting is actually doing it. Consider our best practices for seizing the moment with your employees. In this section, we show you how to level-up the power of complimenting to strengthen relationships. Great compliments usually embody predictable and practical qualities. We recommend you add the following four best practices to your leadership toolbox today.

Sincere compliments strengthen
your leadership influence and your relationships.

Practice 1: Give Compliments Face to Face

There's nothing quite as memorable as a face-to-face moment. This type of communication is by far the most personal way to connect with others. It is the standard against which all other forms of communication are measured. Sending emails or handwritten cards is an effective way to break the ice but usually not sufficient to make a real leadership impact. We were talking with a recognition and employee engagement specialist recently. He said, "Sure, send a card. Send a nice email. But, you've also got to follow up with a face-to-face conversation. . . . That follow up conversation is going to make the recognition feel official and memorable."

Practice 2: Offer Specific Compliments Instead of General Encouragement

General encouragement has limited value. For example, if you say, "Great job on your presentation," the compliment is better than nothing, but it is unlikely to stick. Author and speaker LeeAnn Renniger, who specializes in giving feedback, explained that the centerpiece of all effective feedback is giving a "data point."[12] Data points are concrete examples that illustrate what you mean. If we add some concrete information or data points to the previous message, you will see an immediate difference in the quality of the compliment: "Great job. That was the best presentation I've seen you give. Your main points were really sharp. Your language was clear and concise. I've never seen you more prepared." Another way to add more meaning is to describe the positive outcomes the person created. You might add, for example, "It was really cool to see the way the client leaned forward and became engaged in your message. They really lit up." By adding concrete data to the compliment, you are supersizing the impact.

Practice 3: Give Positive Feedback at Least 80 Percent of the Time

Constructive criticism is unavoidable. That makes it even more important to be deliberate about providing a generous proportion of encouragement. We recommend using the 80/20 rule. That means give positive feedback 80 percent of the time. Think of it like a bank account balance in the relationship. Every compliment is a relationship deposit, and every criticism is a relationship withdrawal. To maintain a good relationship with a healthy balance of support, credibility, and goodwill, you need to offer more positive input than negative input. As business professor and author Kim Cameron explained, "The single most important factor in predicting organizational performance—which was more than twice as powerful as any other fact—was the ratio of positive statements to negative statements."[13] If you emphasize negative feedback too often, the relational bank account quickly gets overdrawn, and that damages the relationship. But if you have cultivated the relationship all along with positive feedback, then difficult conversations, constructive criticism, and hard moments have a positive cushion or margin in the account. Use the 80/20 ratio as your standard and spend most of your time celebrating strengths to prepare for inevitable hard talks.

Practice 4: Take Action

Compliments only count if you give them. We'll explain why we are emphasizing this in a moment. For now, let's take some action as a symbolic step for how you can take action on a day-to-day basis. Take a minute to identify three people you work with. These individuals could be peers, supervisors, or subordinates. Write down their names on a sheet of paper (following the format we outline later) and begin by reflecting on each person's strengths and contributions. Make your compliment as meaningful as possible. Consider these questions to ground your compliment in something concrete:

- When have you seen this employee at their best lately?
- When have you recently seen this employee make a special or important contribution?
- What unique value did they add to the work of the organization?

Once you have written down a compliment for each person, the next step is to deliver it. But here too you have choices to make. See the compliment template in box 4.3 to make your message even more concrete.

Box 4.3. **Compliment Template**

Instructions: Think about your answers to the questions in "Level 4: Put It into Practice." Complete the following talking points to draft a thoughtful compliment for each of the three people you had in mind:

- Name the person:

- What strengths do you see in them?

- Draft your compliment.
  - Give your specific example:

  - Explain the positive outcome of their strengths:

  - Give your specific example:

The first option is to personally deliver the compliment in a one-on-one interaction. This is the face-to-face communication we just mentioned. An easy way to start the conversation is simply to say: "I've been thinking about you lately and wanted to share with you something that has been on my mind." Then deliver the compliment and see how the interaction unfolds. As we have suggested, that's the ultimate approach.

The second option is to express the compliment in a personal note. Grab a card and write down your personalized message. Handwritten notes are great because the recipient can read the message several times and hang it somewhere visible. You can place the note on another person's desk or slip it underneath the door. In fact, some leaders prefer to send a note first and then follow up with a one-on-one conversation to reinforce the message. A leader might say, "Did you get a chance to read my note? I wanted to follow up personally and say how much I appreciate your contributions. I really meant what I said."

The third option is to recognize the employee publicly and share the compliment in a group setting. Doing this consistently creates an overall positive climate. As dean of a college, for instance, Julien started every meeting with "kudos" to celebrate someone's achievements or successes around the college. This consistent agenda item ensured he honored everyone over time. The ideal scenario would be to use all three options: have a conversation, write a note, and recognize the person publicly, all for the same compliment.

Now that you have your three compliments, the most important part is to deliver them. Remember that your thoughts and feelings are important internally, but they have no impact on others unless they are expressed. That's why we emphasize taking action as a best practice.

The most important part of a compliment is communicating it.

As we noted earlier, people often experience resistance to sharing and celebrating others. Celebrating others may make the communicator feel vulnerable. They may believe the compliment won't make a difference or may even make the receiver uncomfortable. As a result, researchers found that "only 50% of people in one experiment who wrote down a compliment for a friend actually sent the compliment along when given the chance, even though they'd already done the hardest part—coming up with something nice and thoughtful to say." Thankfully, our concerns about giving compliments have little basis in fact. Researchers have found that people consistently "underestimate how good their compliment would make the recipient feel." The research shows that "receiving a compliment brightens people's day much more than anticipated, leaving them feeling better, and less uncomfortable, than givers expect."[14]

For today, we encourage you to take action and join the 50 percent of people who did follow up, and deliver the compliment you've prepared one way or another. Now, let's weave complimenting into your team's cultural fabric.

LEVEL 3: BUILD ENGAGEMENT

Positive leaders use compliments frequently and in multiple ways. But leaders can also increase their impact across the entire organization. In this section you'll level up the power of compliments to create a culture in which people are celebrated and implement large-scale practices to increase employee engagement overall. In the spirit of compliments, we advocate for three strategic initiatives to build employee engagement.

Strategic Initiative 1: Measure Employee Engagement

Sitting together via Zoom, we pressed our friend Julie, a director of organizational development, on the importance of communication for people in leadership roles. She slowed down to say: "It. Is. Everything. Most of the problems that you have can be solved with communication." She added, "And most of the problems you have are caused by miscommunication." Communication is key because it's the way that people can connect with each other. "Once you have that connection," she explained, "it's really encouraging and the work happens by itself. Once you have that moment of positive reinforcement, then trust starts to build."

Julie's everyday job is to help her organization create an environment in which employees and patients can thrive. We asked her how she did it. "We had gone through a journey of measuring employee engagement," she said. "We wanted to make sure that employees across departments and teams were connecting with one another, so that they could depend on each other."

To measure employee engagement, Julie and her team turned to Gallup, a group that has studied employee engagement with millions of employees. Put simply, employee engagement reflects people's positive attitudes toward the organization. It includes at least five core elements:[15]

- **Satisfaction**: Do your employees feel satisfied with their experiences at work? Are they frequently recognized for their work? Do they feel close to the people at work? Do they feel that management cares about them?
- **Identification**: Do your employees feel a sense of ownership and pride with the company? Do they feel like they are part of a "we"?
- **Commitment**: Are your employees committed to the mission and values of the organization? Does the organization itself bring them personal meaning?
- **Loyalty**: Do your employees want to be part of this organization long-term? Do they want to spend the rest of their careers here?
- **Performance**: Do your employees regularly exceed expectations? Are they growing and developing? Do they have the opportunity to take on new, challenging, and meaningful tasks?

As a leader, you can take one small step forward by asking yourself these questions. But you can make a giant leap forward by measuring employee engagement concretely in your unit or organization. That's exactly what Julie's organization did. Based on decades of scientific research, Gallup identified twelve questions that will effectively assess an organization's degree of employee engagement. Take a look at these questions and consider what they are measuring. Each item would be answered by choosing one of five options, from strongly agree (1) to strongly disagree (5). Feel free to make a note of the score you would give your organization in your current role.[16]

1. Do you know what is expected of you at work?
2. Do you have the materials and equipment to do your work right?
3. At work, do you have the opportunity to do what you do best every day?
4. In the last seven days, have you received recognition or praise for doing good work?
5. Does your supervisor, or someone at work, seem to care about you as a person?
6. Is there someone at work who encourages your development?
7. At work, do your opinions seem to count?
8. Does the mission/purpose of your company make you feel your job is important?

9. Are your associates (fellow employees) committed to doing quality work?
10. I have a best friend at work.
11. In the last six months, someone at work has talked to me about my progress.
12. This last year, I have had opportunities at work to learn and grow.[17]

Questions 1 and 2 really focus on whether employees have their basic needs met. Do they have clear expectations for doing their jobs, and do they have the resources they need to do their jobs properly? Questions 3, 4, 5, and 6 are all about good management. Notice that one of the key questions is about praise. Questions 7, 8, 9, and 10 are related to a sense of belonging and whether people have good relationships with colleagues at work. The last two questions, 11 and 12, are related to an employee's sense of possibility for growth. Notice that part of that process is receiving feedback frequently. Together, these questions reveal where people are in the organization. The collective scores in each area will help you and your organization make adjustments to better meet the needs of your people.

Use a survey to measure your team members' perceptions and adapt your approach based on the results.

In a recent training, Julien asked a group of top leaders in an organization to take the quick survey for themselves so that they would learn more about the tool. They then looked at the results for the group. In less than five minutes, the whole group learned a great deal. For example, the question that was rated the highest in the group was question 5; most people in the room felt that they had someone who cared about them. This was a really comforting feature of that organization's culture.

The lowest item on the survey, however, was question 11, which focuses on getting regular feedback. A full 62.5 percent of the leadership team who took the survey reported not getting regular feedback. Similarly, low areas were responses to questions 4 and 6, both of which are about the presence of positive communication behaviors, including praise and encouragement. Based on these findings, the leadership team made adjustments to their own practices and developed intentional efforts to improve in those areas. For instance, every leader in the room scheduled a touch-base meeting with their direct reports to see how they were doing and to provide appropriate feedback.

In the same way, you can use these tried-and-true Gallop questions to measure your own employees' level of engagement. This process will give you immediate feedback about your culture, highlight how engaged your employees really are, and offer some areas to celebrate and improve.

Increasing employee engagement, as Julie did, is a long-term marathon, but it has tangible benefits. Researchers have found across studies that having a work environment that fosters positive employee engagement reduces employee turnover, increases customer satisfaction, promotes employee productivity, increases company profit, and lowers absenteeism.[18]

In one study, researchers even found that companies with higher levels of employee engagement experienced higher levels of profits. As the authors explained: "Eight companies that moved from a low level of employee engagement (disengaged) in the first year to the next level (somewhat engaged) the following year showed a 19% average increase in earnings per share; furthermore, two companies that moved from a moderate level of employee engagement in the first year to the highest level of engagement the following year showed a 132% average increase in earnings per shares."[19] In short, not only will you create an environment in which people feel valued and respected, you will also improve your organization's performance. Once you have done that, you need to hire and manage people with their strengths in mind.

Strategic Initiative 2: Hire and Manage for Strengths

A second area of focus is to hire and manage your employees on the basis of their strengths. For many understandable reasons, supervisors often say to themselves, "We have an opening. Who can we get to fill that opening?" We often hire, in other words, simply to fill in a gap, plug a whole, and get the coverage we need. We recommend shifting the mindset to focus on individuals' strengths instead. You can hire this way in the first place. Once you have hired great people, then you can manage people according to their strengths.

In our interview with Julie, she stressed how important it is to capitalize on what people love and enjoy doing rather than on the position. "When you look at someone's strengths," she said, "it takes curiosity as a leader. I think sometimes leaders go wrong when they put their team in a bucket. This one's a data analyst and this one [is in this functional bucket], you know, and these job titles are all that they offer." People, she explained, bring to the table many strengths, and sometimes all they need is an opportunity to reveal them.

Julie gave us her bottom line: "As a leader, you're there to serve the people who are on your team." That means you have to get to know them. Julie added, "Whatever time that takes." Look for special strengths that are totally unique to each person compared to everyone else on the team. You might even notice that certain activities get them excited or that they seem to enjoy certain tasks rather than others. "You see that look [in their eyes]," Julie explained, "and you have a conversation with them. 'What did you love the most here because your eyes are shining? You are like on fire.'"

Once she has identified that special area of strength and passion, Julie probes more deeply and becomes even more curious, "Tell me exactly what you liked about that? Tell me what pieces of this task got you the most excited?" Once you've explored this with your employee, you keep it on record, and as opportunities arise, you tap into that person's natural talent.

When you focus on your employees' strengths,
you will naturally improve employee engagement because
you are making decisions based on what people do best.

Once you start managing your employees based on their strengths, interactions in your unit will change. Julie gave us concrete examples of how this plays out. "For me, it [became] very natural to say 'I have a colleague that is really good at this. So, I want them to spend as much time as is possible on this task she loves." Then a butterfly effect influenced the entire team. "Collectively," Julie said, "we would sit down and say, 'Okay, she really loves doing this type of work and we have a need for it, but we've got to take something off her plate.'" She energized her team by talking about tasks and responsibilities based on the strengths her team members all brought to the table. Her team now engages in conversations about their projects the same way. Julie replayed what she's heard her team members say, "I'll trade you because I don't want to do this. I don't like doing this part, but I'll take that if you want to take that." Julie conceded, "It was a hot mess for a while," but then "it worked out beautifully."

When you focus on your employees' strengths, you will naturally improve employee engagement because you are organizing a system that is based on what people love to do and do best. When people are passionate about their projects, they want to shine and show what they can do. By identifying and organizing around their strengths, you're tapping into their potential excellence.

Strategic Initiative 3: Start a Recognition Program

The third strategy we recommend is creating your own recognition program. There are many ways of cultivating employee engagement, including supporting work-life balance, providing opportunities for your employees to grow and develop professionally, encouraging health and safety, and getting them engaged. But as we have shown throughout the chapter, one core practice is to offer compliments, praise, and recognition for your employees' contributions.

Researchers have shown that well-designed recognition programs can have a significant impact. Organizations that used recognition as part of their organizational development approach experienced an average of 15 percent performance improvement.[20] Further, as mentioned at the opening of the chapter, a group of companies with the most effective programs "provided a 91% return to shareholders."[21] When done well, investments in recognition programs are about as close as you can come to a sure bet.

There are lots of great examples for how to start your own recognition program. Travel Related Services (TRS), for instance, initiated a successful program called "Great Performers." It was done quite simply by first displaying life-sized posters of famous people performing at their best. These posters were placed throughout the company for many weeks. Then the company used pictures of actual TRS employees, with a statement of a major accomplishment for each employee. They gave their employees the star treatment, and the effects were tremendous. The program helped to increase the company's net income by 500 percent over an eleven-year period.[22]

In another example, Julie launched a very successful program at her organization called the "Best Champion Program." First, employees across the organization were nominated for the program as standout employees. Julie said, "People were nominated by their peers, so that alone is big. It's a mood booster." Once a month, Julie gathered the group of over two hundred individuals, celebrated each of them, and asked for their advice. "We were engaging them in the process of how to improve our organization," she explained.

The organization invested in them by bringing in special keynote speakers, providing professional development opportunities for them, and celebrating their accomplishments in fun ways. The Best Champions became influential leaders in their departments. Julie explained, "They're the people who are always stepping up." In a ripple effect, the honored employees became cultural energizers for the organization. "They made a real difference," Julie concluded. See box 4.4 to examine your own recognition program.

Recognition must be done sincerely and well. By developing a formal recognition program, you will build into your culture a tacit understanding that employees are valued and respected. You will inspire your employees

---

Box 4.4. **Designing Your Own Recognition Program**

Instructions: Recognition programs can take many forms. You can adapt an existing program or design your own. Be as creative as you and your team want to be. Researchers have found, however, that several key characteristics are needed for such a program to be successful. If you already have a recognition program, check any of the following boxes that apply:

- ☐ Your recognition is immediate and personal.
- ☐ You are committing financial and personal resources (such as your time).
- ☐ You are connecting the program with your organization's needs, expectations, and performance measures.
- ☐ You are working with your employees to give them ownership of the program and to make sure the recognition and incentives are in line with their needs. As researchers Daniel and Metcalf explained, "A recognition system begins to falter when employees start thinking that their actions are being insulted by inconsequential incentives."[1]
- ☐ You keep it simple.
- ☐ You assess the impact of your initiative on concrete outcomes.[2]

Notes

1. Daniel, T. A., & Metcalf, G. S. (2005). The fundamentals of employee recognition. *Society of Human Resource Management, 1*, 7.
2. Daniel. T. A., & Metcalf, G. S. (2005). The fundamentals of employee recognition. *Society of Human Resource Management, 1*, 7.

to thrive, connect with the values of the organization, and create a positive workplace environment for the entire organization. Recognition programs are thus an essential part of your toolbox to engage your employees and create a culture that is based on trust and strength.

LEVEL 4: PUT IT INTO PRACTICE

Let's distill these ideas into some concrete action steps so you'll be more likely to put them into practice. As a leader, what steps can you take to build the act of complimenting into your leadership approach and daily habits? Consider the following takeaways and circle those that you would most like to put into practice.

The Power of Compliments

- **Compliments are like a mirror.** First, fully appreciate the power of compliments, praise, and positive feedback in shaping other's self-perceptions. Then give compliments to shape the way others see themselves.
- **Express the strengths you see in others.** Identify the best of what you see in others and communicate the strengths you see in them.
- **Meaningful compliments make memorable moments.** Recognize that leaders are uniquely positioned to offer compliments that really stick. Are you using your position of strength as a positive authority figure to compliment others in ways they need to hear? The influence of some compliments lasts a lifetime.
- **Overcome your resistance to giving compliments.** The benefits of sincere compliments are quantifiable. If you still hesitate to offer positive praise, we encourage you to identify and overcome your resistance to giving compliments. Your resistance might be holding your team back from being its best.

Strengthen Relationships with These Best Compliment Practices

- **Compliments are best given face to face.** There is no real substitute for face-to-face connections. It's the most personal and powerful way to give compliments. A face-to-face conversation makes the compliment personal, memorable, and official.

- **Specific compliments have more impact than general encouragement.** Be sure to add concrete details or "data" to your compliments. Explain the specifics of the strengths and positive qualities you see in others.
- **Give positive feedback at least 80 percent of the time.** Use a banking metaphor for the proportion of feedback you give. Positive feedback makes deposits in your relationship accounts. Negative, corrective, or constructive feedback makes withdrawals. Positive feedback has lots of benefits and also gives you room to have more difficult conversations when needed.
- **Take action.** Think of three people on or around your team. Identify one strength you see in each person. Write out a specific compliment. Then take action and deliver the compliment face-to-face, with a written note, or in a public setting. Better yet, do all three to create maximum impact.

Get Serious about Engagement and Recognition for Your Organization

- **Measure employee engagement.** For starters, we recommend using Gallop's twelve employee engagement questions. Collect the data from your team members, analyze the results, and make changes in the areas that would have the greatest impact. When done periodically, using data about employee engagement will ensure that you continue to communicate positively, develop your skills, and build accountability.
- **Hire and manage for strengths.** Recalibrate your hiring and delegation process around people's strengths. Become a "talent scout" for the strengths of every member of your team. Find out what tasks and projects "get their motors running" and then match the projects and assignments with people's natural abilities.
- **Start a recognition program.** Recognition programs are limited only by your imagination. But the best program is the one you'll actually use. Whatever approach you take, make sure it is done well, done sincerely, and done in a way that makes a real difference for your team members.

CONCLUSION

In this chapter you have learned about the power of compliments, best practices to strengthen your relationships, and ways to engage your entire organization in the process. When taken seriously, compliments, praise, and positive feedback can truly transform your leadership approach and your team's culture. Employee engagement affects employee safety, health, happiness, productivity, and quality of work. But in the end, it is a commitment you decide to make as a leader. It's a decision about how you direct your attention and efforts toward others.

Our advice is simple: Use every opportunity you have to strengthen your employees, build them up, and prepare them for their future.

Complimenting needs to be a top priority in times of both struggle and success. Anne Ricketts, the executive coach we mentioned earlier, shared a story about a director who struggled with giving positive feedback and lost several top performers because of it. As a result, she vowed to change her approach. In one instance, she found a way to keep a tradition of compliments alive. Anne explains the director's situation. "Every year, her team hosted a holiday party. I reminded her to take the time to go around and say something nice about every single person and to be specific. The team really appreciated the tradition."

"As the team got bigger and grew to over 20 people," Anne continued, the director "thought there wouldn't be enough time and it would be challenging to say something specific about each team member. She only directly supervised the four team managers under her and the opportunities for regular interactions with some team members were limited, especially when working remotely. Nevertheless, the team members still wanted positive affirmation and wanted to keep the holiday tradition alive. As the director, her solution was to talk positively about the four managers she supervised and then asked those four managers ahead of time to prepare to take turns saying something complimentary about each of the team members they directly supervised."

This simple solution preserved the tradition of complimenting and played an important part in the director's broader efforts to turn around her leadership and team's culture by providing regular positive feedback, recognition, and praise. See box 4.5 to commit to your own next steps.

Positive leaders compliment to affect others' personal growth.

Box 4.5.   **Top Takeaways**

Reflecting on your selections in the "Level 4: Put It into Practice" section, what are your top three takeaways?

1.

2.

3.

5

Disclose to Deepen Relationships

Several years ago, Julien interviewed Valerie, a leading scholar in the field of communication. She'd studied and taught communication her entire adult life but struggled with being herself and revealing who she really was in relationships. She had lost friends, colleagues, and many opportunities to share and connect with others over the years. She said, "I never knew the extent to which my own fear was coming across as not being open or as being reticent. And that is not a very engaging way to be."[1] Valerie's story illustrates a common problem for leaders. As the saying goes, "It's lonely at the top." Researchers reported that 52 percent of CEOs frequently feel lonely and that small business owners consistently experience a "pervasive sense of loneliness."[2] Loneliness for leaders is associated with poor health, depression, and feelings of helplessness. What leads to this loneliness is simple. As one researcher explained, "Leadership positions within organizations often do not foster work environments where friendship and social intimacy are possible."[3]

One main reason leaders experience loneliness is the self-imposed social distance many executives maintain. Valerie admits, for instance, that she'd been withdrawn and unwilling to engage authentically on her side of conversations. Once she realized this, Valerie pursued a new way of communicating. She decided to move in the direction of others and allowed her relationships to deepen. She opened up and made it safe for others to do so.

In this chapter you'll learn to be more authentic and open in ways that will deepen your relationships and enhance your leadership. You'll learn the fourth principle of positive communication: **when you disclose, you naturally deepen the relationships that you have with others.** First, you'll learn the power of disclosing and how it can help you as a leader. Second, you'll learn to disclose in ways that strengthen your relationships at work. Third, you'll level up these skills and create a safe environment for all.

LEVEL 1: THE POWER OF DISCLOSING

At a basic level, disclosure is about revealing aspects of yourself others would not know about unless you told them. But that's not all there is to it. Disclosure involves an endless number of small actions that reveal who you are, what you think, and how you feel over time. For relationships to be deepened, disclosure needs to include certain basic features:

√ It must be authentic and genuine.
√ It must be truthful and honest.
√ It must be spontaneous rather than calculated.
√ It must be personal.
√ It must reflect a shared human experience.

Disclosure plays out much more powerfully in real life than this list of basics might suggest. Consider what positive disclosure looks like in action.

Nick Saban is one of the greatest college football coaches of all time. He has won seven national championships and ten SEC championships. But in 2022, Alabama lost the championship crown to Georgia. In the postgame press conference, Saban answered numerous questions. Two of his top players, Bryce Young and Will Anderson Jr., sat beside him. Journalists asked questions about the loss, and Saban gave surprisingly authentic answers. As the two players stood up to leave, Nick asked them nonverbally to sit down. He said: "I'd like to say something. Can I say something?" "Absolutely," the person managing the press conference replied. Here's what Coach Saban said:

> These two guys sitting up here, they're not defined by one game. They played great for us all year, they were great competitors, great leaders on this team and they contributed tremendously to the success of this team. And we would

not be here without them. And both of them take responsibility for the loss, but both of them contributed in a lot of ways, in a positive way, to giving us a chance to win and a chance to be here to have an opportunity to win. I just want to thank them for that and let everyone know how proud I am of these two guys.[4]

Saban took the conversation outside of the stereotypical role coaches often play in a public press conference. He disclosed authentically, and that clearly touched his players. The players both stood up after these words. And although many people would miss this small behavior, right before they left the stage, both players reached out with their hands and touched the coach on his shoulders from either side. It was the players' way of saying thank you for the spontaneous, kind, and supportive words. Saban spoke from the heart. That made all the difference. Authentic disclosure like this changes leaders' relationship dynamics in powerful ways.

There are many moments in which leaders may feel tempted to keep their "game face" on and play a role. However, these are often the exact moments when courageous leaders will disclose authentically. When you disclose authentically and express your thoughts and feelings, you strengthen your relationships.

Positive communication is not about pretending, manipulating, or controlling others. It's all about connecting more deeply with people, but it also involves risks. Leaders like Coach Saban have no guarantees that others will receive their message well or respond positively. That's why disclosure consists of vulnerability and courage in equal parts, as Brené Brown, author of *Daring Greatly*, explained. She wrote that vulnerability means, in part, "uncertainty, risks, and emotional exposure."[5] Openness and vulnerability are not signs of weakness, rather, they are key measures of our courage. To help move in this direction, we propose five habits of disclosure that will have a long-term impact on your leadership.

When you disclose authentically and express your thoughts and feelings, you strengthen your relationships.

Habit 1: Share Your Story

One way of deepening relationships is to take the initiative to share information about your personal experiences and professional journey. Sharing your story makes a positive difference across contexts. For example, in health-care settings, doctors who reveal their own experiences improve patient satis-faction, increase patient adherence to treatment, and decrease the likelihood of being sued.[6] In education, teachers who share their experiences, academic hardships, and even professional struggles increase their students' learning.[7] That's because sharing your story creates more trust and better working rela-tionships. As one recent study found in the context of small working groups, "revealing personal information encourages others to do the same, thereby facilitating mutual exchange of personal information between teammates [and it] improves the quality of relationship they have with each other."[8]

There are many ways to share your story. You could, for example, start a meeting with something personal such as talking about a moment from your weekend that gave you joy. You might also want to tell stories about your hardships, challenges, weaknesses, and mistakes. See box 5.1 for some easy-to-use strategies. This may feel counterintuitive, but the research is clear: "Disclosing personal information and revealing weaknesses provides room for mutual trust to develop which, in turn, encourages teammates to feel free (and safe) to express themselves."[9]

In his work, author and executive coach Allen Weiner wrote about how talking about our weaknesses or "foibles" can help create better connections and make it feel safer for others to do the same. Weiner explained, "A foible is a small weakness. . . . When I talk about mine, people talk about theirs.

Box 5.1. How to Talk about Weaknesses

Talking about small mistakes and weaknesses is a great starting place. If you are feeling especially courageous, share major shortcomings, mistakes, or life struggles. You may be surprised at how hungry your workplace culture is for open communication.

Check any of the following boxes that apply to you:

- ☐ I reveal difficult moments I've faced.
- ☐ I reveal both positive and negative experiences I've had throughout my professional career.
- ☐ I connect with others through open discussion. For example, if an employee shares that they have lost someone close to them and this is something I have also experienced, I take a moment to reciprocate and share my story.

Sometimes that helps us make a connection. I think I've surprised a lot of people by my willingness to share a weakness, and it's helped them open up to me. The more 'unsuitable' my weakness–to a point–the more I've invited such a connection. Most of the time, the person I've been talking with [about my weakness] will say, 'Don't be so hard on yourself. I can get you one better.'"[10]

Habit 2: Reveal Your Emotions and Thoughts

A second way of practicing disclosure is to reveal your thoughts and emotions transparently. Part of what decreases our connection with others is our temptation to hide how we truly feel or what we think. When we put on a mask and play a role, it's difficult for other people to know where we stand. It's helpful to remember that emotions are human. Emotions are not the problem. The way we handle them is.

One suggestion is this: find a way to express the emotion that you are feeling by completing the statement: "I feel . . ." with a statement of the actual emotion. Consider some examples:

- "I feel very *pleased* that we're making such great progress."
- "I feel *happy* about the success of our training."
- "I feel *frustrated* that we were not able to meet our objectives this quarter."
- "I feel a lot of *disappointment* about the breakdown in communication that is taking place across the organization."

Notice that in each example we are simply stating the emotion we are experiencing using "I" language. We are not criticizing, blaming, or focusing on other people. We are stating how *we* feel. That allows us to express ourselves without putting other people on the defensive.

Identifying and stating your emotions clearly will help others understand you. This shows others that who you are inwardly matches how you express yourself outwardly. As Carl Rogers put it, when somebody speaks authentically, "we recognize that he not only means exactly what he says, but that his deepest feelings also match what he is expressing."[11] The ability to communicate congruently is at the heart of effective leadership. It decreases uncertainty, builds trust, and is a risk worth taking.

Clarifying our thoughts can be just as constructive. In the book *Crucial Conversations*, Joseph Grenny and his colleagues explained an effective approach to difficult conversations. The sequence of actions they offered begins with a three-part structure: start with facts, tell your story, and ask for their view.[12]

Imagine, for instance, that you need to talk to an employee about being at work on time. For two weeks they have been coming to work late, and it is becoming an issue. Conversations like these can be tricky. How could you approach this discussion effectively?

1. **State your facts.** Simply share what you have been observing in the problematic behavior: "In the last two weeks, I have noticed that you have been coming to work late. So far this week, you've arrived twenty minutes late on both Monday and Tuesday."

2. **Share your story.** This means sharing your stance and your thinking. You might say, "Being on time is critical for your position because our customers depend on you, and so do we. I also need your support in the office. When you are not present, I am not able to fulfill my responsibilities."

3. **Finally, finish by asking for their perspective.** (Remember chapter 3 about asking questions?) Your goal is to share the floor of the conversation, to ask for input, and to seek to understand. You could ask: "This is typically not like you. Is there something going on that is preventing you from being on time?"

If you have handled conversations like this, then you've revealed your thoughts in a composed and professional way. You have started a difficult conversation on the right foot.

Habit 3: Set Proper Expectations

Similarly, leaders should communicate transparently about their expectations. Your people cannot read your mind. In 2019, Julien got a new boss, the provost and executive vice chancellor at the university. In the first week on the job, the new provost set an initial meeting with her direct reports. She came into the room on time, smiling and with pep in her step. Facing the team, she began with introductions and small talk and shared the agenda for the meeting. "The first item on our agenda," she said, "is to share my expectations." Her executive assistant then passed around a single handout listing twelve expectations.

"Let me explain my expectations clearly so that we can all be on the same page," she said professionally. Then she patiently explained each expectation and provided concrete examples. Coming back from the meeting, Julien took the handout and pinned it on a board next to his desk. "I know what to do now," he thought.

Some followers thrive no matter what, but a lot of the daily frustrations that come with leading a team occur when people do not meet your expectations. The flipside of this coin is that we know many supervisors who do not clearly communicate their expectations in the first place.

Setting clear expectations builds trust, establishes an honest professional relationship, and helps your team members succeed.

Many leaders feel as if their followers should already know what is expected of them. One of our friends, Ben, is director of a large unit for an international nongovernmental organization. "One of my major frustrations," he said, "is that people on my team are not taking initiative. This is a huge time suck for me." He added, "I have to check in with people, tell them what I need to get done, and then keep track of what they have done and not done. . . . I talked to the team, but nothing has changed." When we probed more deeply, he explained that he didn't express his expectations clearly. Like many leaders, he talked in passing about his general expectations at one meeting, but he didn't write anything down and didn't explain any concrete outcomes or clear action steps he was looking for.

To remedy the situation, we encouraged Ben to go back to the basics:

- Write down the expectations clearly.
- Distribute those expectations to the team in an official meeting.
- Identify specific concrete actions for each expectation.

For instance, one of Ben's expectations was that he wanted his followers to take the initiative. He spelled out what taking the initiative meant: (a) volunteering to lead a special project, (b) providing an update on an action item that has been agreed upon, or (c) reporting a problem or a delay immediately. Once he had clearly communicated his expectations like this, Ben was in a much better position to coach his staff, hold people accountable, and address performance issues.

One reason we often do not share our expectations clearly is that we assume people know what we know and think like we think. We also assume that all our employees will, or at least *should*, perform at the highest level without guidance. Leaders may also shy away from setting expectations because they don't want the conversation to feel awkward or to disturb harmonious relationships. For us, setting clear expectations with a supportive and professional attitude is positive communication. See box 5.2 to prepare concrete

---

Box 5.2. **Set your Expectations**

Instructions: Developing clear expectations is critical for employee performance and for reducing unnecessary conflicts. Take a moment to make a list of your top five expectations for the workplace. Write down each expectation in a concise sentence. Complete this statement: "I expect that my employees will . . ."

- Expectation 1:

- Expectation 2:

- Expectation 3:

- Expectation 4:

- Expectation 5:

Once you have written down clear expectations, prepare clear and concrete examples and illustrations. Next, set up a meeting with your team to share them. Be cautious to not deliver your message with a heavy-handed tone. Instead, approach the conversation with respect, gratitude, and professionalism.

expectations for your team. It builds trust, establishes an honest professional relationship, and helps your team members succeed. Nobody likes hearing about their failure to meet expectations that were never communicated in the first place. Your followers will appreciate being given clear targets.

Habit 4: Express Your Gratitude

Disclosure also means expressing our gratitude. In his landmark work, *A Small Treatise on the Great Virtues*, the French philosopher Andre Comte-Sponville wrote, "Gratitude is a gift, gratitude is sharing, gratitude is love."[13] We feel gratitude when we understand that other people have contributed to our development. As a virtue, gratitude calls on us to realize that our well-being, our accomplishments, and our success are always shared and depends on others' help.

Expressing gratitude has numerous benefits for the communicator.[14] It accomplishes the following:

- √ Strengthens our sense of connection.
- √ Increases the comfort we feel with others.
- √ Reduces depression.
- √ Is associated with fewer symptoms of physical illness.
- √ Leads to more exercise.

- √ Helps people sleep better.
- √ Contributes to greater happiness and life satisfaction.
- √ Helps us feel more optimistic.
- √ Increases prosocial behavior.
- √ Produces positive effects lasting up to six months after deliberately expressing gratitude.

For leaders, expressing gratitude serves many purposes. At the risk of stating the obvious, as Kim Cameron put it, "People demonstrate significantly higher performance at work when a positive climate exists."[15] Still, our point here is not first and foremost to express gratitude merely to increase performance. Gratitude will help you navigate the world of relationships, encourage stronger connectedness, and facilitate a positive climate.

The channels for expressing gratitude are essentially the same as those we encouraged you to use for compliments (see chapter 4): you can do it one on one, with a handwritten note, or publicly in a group setting. Regardless of the channel, expressing gratitude needs to be at the heart of your toolkit for positive communication. You can even do it right now by taking our gratitude challenge in box 5.3.

> ## Box 5.3. **The Gratitude Challenge**
>
> **Instructions:** Take a moment to think of someone you are working with for whom you are grateful. Identify someone you could text right now. Once you are ready, prepare a text message for this person using these lead-in prompts:
>
> - Start like this: "I have been thinking of you and wanted to tell you . . ."
> - Next, give one or more specific examples of what you are grateful for.
> - Finish your message with a direct statement of gratitude: ". . . how grateful I am for the great work you have been doing on this project and for the support you are providing to this team."
>
> Once you have written the message, press send. Right before pressing the button, you might feel a small moment of hesitation. What you are feeling is very likely a sense of vulnerability. That's the feeling that comes with taking a risk. Now, be courageous and press send anyway.

LEVEL 2: REINFORCE RELATIONSHIPS

One common misconception about positive communication is that leaders need to be "happy-go-lucky" types and shy away from potentially difficult conversations. We disagree. Positive communication is about finding a way forward by engaging with excellence in difficult, challenging, and honest conversations. Practicing positive leadership is about learning to bridge the gap between the difficult situations we face and the techniques we use to respond. In this section you'll level up by learning specific tools and techniques to manage those difficult moments. When you handle these situations well, you will often see your relationships strengthen and deepen.

Technique 1: Break the Ice with Purpose

One major issue at work is a feeling of isolation. During the COVID-19 pandemic, many organizations adapted quickly and made it possible for employees to work remotely. Technologies like Zoom or Google Teams have clear benefits. However, in our postpandemic world, many professionals still report feeling distant from one another and are unable to find points of connection.

For example, we recently led a training for a large international nonprofit organization. It was the first time in almost two years those employees had met in person. Numerous team members had come and gone during that time. As a result, many employees knew little about one another and felt isolated and alone. As in many organizations, this team got right to task-related conversations just moments after the video meetings started. After all, it feels less natural to make small talk, swap stories, or share laughter on camera. For people to work well together, however, they need lots of opportunities for connection regardless of the communication channel.

One effective way to create connections in meetings is to plan for icebreakers that encourage appropriate disclosure. Many icebreakers can feel a bit random or lack purpose other than lightening the mood. Leaders, however, can create an intentional moment at the start of the meeting during which people have a chance to have fun and get to know each other. This takes more planning for video calls, but many options are available to open up the meeting purposefully.

One exercise that is especially helpful in promoting disclosure is an icebreaker called *highlight-hero-hardship*. In this icebreaker, you simply ask every member of your team to first share a highlight, something that is going well in their personal or professional life. Next, the person shares a hero of the week, someone who has had a positive impact on them. Once again, that person can be in their personal life or at work. Finally, the person shares a hardship they are facing, whether it is occurring at work or at home.

This exercise promotes a well-balanced approach to disclosure. It helps each person around the table focus on a positive experience at work. It gives them an opportunity to feel and express gratitude for someone who is having an impact. And finally, it builds empathy about people's experiences by understanding a hardship they are facing. The added value for the leader is tremendous: it creates cohesion and connection among the group. It gives you a chance to personally recognize heroes if they are from the workplace. And it provides understanding about how your employees are doing and creates opportunities to help them solve problems.

In short, use the power of disclosure to create conversations in which people can share more of who they are and their experiences. Make a habit of breaking the ice at meetings with purpose to strengthen those relationships. We show you how in box 5.4.

Box 5.4. **Effective Icebreakers**

Instructions: Here is a list of five easy-to-use icebreakers. Put a check mark next to the exercise you will use at your next team meeting and then put it on the agenda.

- ☐ *Highlight-hero-hardship*: Each person shares something that is going well in their lives, a hero who is making a difference in their lives, and something that is difficult for them.
- ☐ *Two truths and a lie:* Speakers share three facts about themselves, but one of them is a lie. The rest of the team has to guess which are true and which are false.
- ☐ *Show and tell over Zoom:* Show a meaningful object for the camera on Zoom and explain its significance.
- ☐ *Birth map:* Use map software and ask each person to show the group where they were born and raised.
- ☐ *Meet my pet:* Ask each person to either show their pet via Zoom or bring one to work that day.

For an even more effective strategy, ask each team member to be responsible for the icebreaker for a following meeting.

Technique 2: Clarify What You Really Want

In their blockbuster bestseller *Crucial Conversations*, the authors wrote that changes in human relationships "begin with your heart."[16] Difficult conversations tend to pull us in different directions. On the one hand, we may have the impulse to shy away from the conversation. This is our flight response. Another impulse is to fight, to become more aggressive and direct and to focus entirely on "winning" the conversation regardless of the damage done. Unfortunately, neither flight nor fight creates constructive outcomes. We have to start somewhere else.

For example, we recently received an email from someone who needed advice. This person was leading a large department that was going through a difficult season. "Tomorrow at 1 p.m., I need to give someone feedback [about a person]," she explained, "and it's the start of a three-year working relationship. . . . I'm struggling with the delivery of my message and how to position this information through positive communication." She had past experiences with this person and was concerned about the emotional baggage she might bring into the conversation.

As we learned more, it became clear that her initial impulse for approaching the conversation wasn't going to work. When we are angry or upset, we most often focus on the other person's faults. We make accusations, criticize, and attack the person's character rather than focusing on the problematic behavior itself. In the end, this approach hurts relationships, erodes trust, and makes further interaction even more difficult.

To help with this situation, we drew on an approach from *Crucial Conversations*. The authors call it "Starting with Heart," and it all begins with three fundamental questions:

- What do I really want for myself?
- What do I really want for others?
- What do I really want for the relationship?

Once you have answered these questions, you need to ask a fourth one: "What should I do right now to move toward what I really want?"

In the conversation, the leader successfully moved away from the accusations and criticisms that had previously swirled in her head. Instead, she expressed *what she wanted to see* happening and that she wanted a good relationship with her new hire in an affirmative way. At the same time, she provided some feedback about what she needed from him moving forward, namely that she needed him to protect her time by scheduling meeting times appropriately. The hardest part of this conversation was taking the time to clarify what she wanted in the first place.

Technique 3: Use the "What I Need from You" (WINFY) Approach

To have meaningful conversations, you sometimes need to slow down the process of communication. During back-and-forth conversations, we often feel forced to answer immediately. The more upset we are, the more quickly we tend to respond. We may end up saying things hastily that make matters worse.

A better approach is to recognize that the interaction is speeding up and deliberately slow it down by using the WINFY method, or "What I need from you." WINFY is one of many excellent techniques developed by Henri Lipmanowicz and Keith McCandless that are designed to open up conversation and drive innovation in organizations. Several years ago, Julien used WINFY in one especially meaningful interaction.[17]

Christina and Julien are wonderful friends now. Over time, they became powerful allies. This wasn't always the case. For three years, Christina served as director of development for the same college Julien served as dean. In these roles, they were expected to work as collaborative peers on certain projects but faced some challenges early in their professional relationship. Individually, they are both hard workers, positive people, smart, passionate, value driven, and mission centered. But they are both competitive and self-reliant. They struggled to become interdependent, to rely on one another, trust each other, and respect each other's views. A team cannot function in this way.

They were essentially pretending to get along, but their relationship was stuck and so were their projects. How could they be emotionally honest in a professional relationship without saying something hurtful to each other?

They decided to use WINFY at a yearly planning retreat.

WINFY is very simple to use. It is ideal for a two-person conversation. First, each person takes about five minutes to complete the statement in box 5.5.

Box 5.5.

What I need from you is _____.

During this five-minute period, each person individually brainstorms several needs that are important to them, then narrows their focus to the top one or two needs. It's important to write down the needs. The act of putting something on paper is therapeutic. Once each person has identified their core needs, they share them with the other person, who then has a chance to respond and express whether this is a need they can meet.

As Julien and Christina sat in a coffee shop preparing for the next semester, they used WINFY to jumpstart the retreat. Christina reflected on what she needed most and wrote it down. Julien did the same. They then shared what they had written.

When Christina began, she said, "What I need from you is for you to trust me." Julien listened to her statement and even wrote it down. After a few back-and-forth talking turns to clarify, he then expressed his own need: "What I need from you is to involve me and to respect me." She wrote that down, listened, and processed the statement.

This conversation was a true turning point. WINFY is a simple exercise that deepened their understanding of one another. As a result of this conversation, they truly joined forces for the first time and became a powerful fundraising team who enjoyed working together. They even called themselves "the dream team," competed in tennis tournaments together to raise funds for the college, and ultimately raised millions of dollars to benefit students. They also became good friends.

What makes WINFY so powerful is its simplicity. The WINFY exercise gives people the opportunity to express what they are often unable to share because frustrations and criticisms are clouding the real issue: Our needs are not being met. That's the core issue. When we express our needs, we are not criticizing or complaining. This exercise helps us simply state what we need.

Technique 4: Apologize for Missteps

Part of disclosure means being open about our missteps. A few years ago, we were coaching a senior vice president (SVP) and board member of an engineering firm. For many years the executive was a beloved leader. He fought for his people, brought new business to the company, and was exceptionally successful. He aspired to follow in the footsteps of his mentor and become the next CEO. When he was passed over for the position, however, he started creating unnecessary tension with his colleagues. His once positive relationships took a turn for the worse. When he described to us his last 12 months, he labeled difficult incidents as strikes: "Strike 1" (not getting the promotion), "Strike 2" (creating tension with fellow board members), and "Strike 3" (creating tension with the new CEO). He knew he had seriously damaged his credibility, and his career was now on thin ice. He was motivated to turn it around. Together, he and Julien worked on a plan to rebuild his relationships.

A powerful moment came when he wrote a memo to his stakeholders to avoid further misrepresentations and possible conflicts. He wanted a letter to alleviate tension and demonstrate goodwill. He revised the language several times and finally got the courage to include this: "I take full responsibility for this and I simply apologize." He sent the email to all relevant stakeholders. At our next meeting, he told us: "I have to tell you, apologizing was the hardest part of the letter for me. I almost sent it without it." He was glad he had included the apology. The response from people was amazing. He received kind notes from his people, his colleagues, and even his boss. They labeled it a "leadership moment."

The team's response should not come as a surprise. As researchers have shown in several case studies, "apologies are critical in rebuilding and sustaining long-term relationships" and play vital leadership functions. The letter and the apology helped the SVP regain his credibility, influence, and positive relationships with the board and his new boss.

---

*A sincere apology is often the only way
to clear the air and move forward.*

Of course we do not suggest you apologize unless you have done something wrong. A principled disagreement with another person does not require an apology even if they are taken aback. Likewise, don't apologize just because somebody has pointed the finger at you. Apologies for actual errors happen too infrequently in organizations. Many people avoid apologies because they feel they are a sign of weakness, will expose them to litigation, or will cost them the support of stakeholders. This is seldom the case. A sincere apology is often the *only* way to clear the air and move forward. That's why many people see a good apology as a demonstration of leadership. As Erika Andersen, the founding partner of Proteus International, said, "When someone truly apologizes, we know he or she is putting honesty and honor above personal comfort or self-protection. It's inspiring, and it feels brave."[18]

You may also have noticed that when some people do apologize, they often only go part of the way. They might admit that a mistake happened but never sincerely say "I'm sorry" or "I apologize." Even worse, some people will use an insincere apology to confuse the situation, "I'm sorry that *you* are upset" or "I regret that it happened, but you made me so angry . . . ." These partial or phony apologies are likely to hurt our credibility and ability to lead others. If you've made a mistake or have done something wrong, we recommend accepting full responsibility and apologizing well.

Instructions: To prepare for an effective apology, we recommend an approach with four major steps.[1]

Step 1	**Name the Mistake and Take Full Responsibility** "I take full responsibility for . . ." ". . . was my mistake." "I was wrong to . . ."
Step 2	**Apologize and Express Remorse** "I apologize for causing this . . ." "I'm sorry that I handled this poorly." "Please accept my apology for . . ." "I regret the harm that my actions have caused, and I am sorry."
Step 3	**Say What You'll Do to Solve the Problem** "It won't happen again. Here are the steps I'll be taking: . . ." "I've cleared my calendar today to fix this." "I will do better next time because . . ."
Step 4	**Follow through with Concrete Action**

Apologies are an important step in wiping the slate clean, and they position others to forgive you, let go of the past, and move forward together.

Note

1. Tucker, S., Turner, N., Barling, J., Reid, E. M., & Elving, C. (2006). Apologies and transformational leadership. *Journal of Business Ethics*, 63(2), 195–207.

We hope you see that positive communication, and, in particular, disclosure, is not all about being "warm and fuzzy." Disclosure is a huge challenge for many people. It often requires taking a courageous, deep breath and having difficult conversations skillfully. Once you know how to do it, you are ready to make it safe for others to do the same.

LEVEL 3: MAKE IT SAFE FOR OTHERS TO SPEAK UP

Disclosing is a powerful way for leaders to show who they are and to strengthen relationships. It's also crucial to creating a healthy culture. The recent demands for transparency, openness, and the ability to "speak up" at work underscore the importance of disclosure when it comes to the practical, task-driven side of the work we do. One key sign of a healthy culture is when leaders disclose important information freely. But this is not always the norm. Secrecy is a common element in countless corporate scandals or disasters, including Enron's infamous accounting fraud and insider trading scandal; the Boy Scouts of America sexual abuse lawsuits; and the recent case of Elizabeth Holmes, former CEO of Theranos, who was convicted of numerous cases of fraud for misleading investors in her company.[19]

Look at virtually any large organizational disaster. The common thread is that leaders established a norm of secrecy rather than promoting open and transparent disclosure. Let's face it, as Aflac CEO Dan Amos once said, "Bad news does not improve with age."[20] When leaders don't create a norm of disclosure or a "speak-up environment," things quickly unravel.

NASA's two space shuttle explosions illustrate what can happen when it's not safe to speak up.[21] In the 1960s and 1970s, NASA established open lines of communication in a network that allowed anyone to talk to anyone about emerging safety issues or other concerns. At the time, the system of checks and balances was relatively healthy, facilitated rapid identification of problems and their solutions, and allowed NASA to put humans on the moon. In that era, NASA was known for its discipline and life-saving protocols. After all, part of John F. Kennedy's "moon speech" vision was not just landing a man on the moon but also "returning him *safely* to Earth."

Unfortunately, by the time of the *Challenger* explosion years later in 1986, NASA's culture had changed. Information flowed down the chain of command but not up. Top-down messages were treated as military-like "orders."

The mechanisms for speaking up had gone extinct. Just prior to both shuttle explosions—the *Challenger* in 1986 and *Columbia* in 2003—the same dysfunctional communication symptoms showed up in each disaster.

In both cases, numerous levels of managers refused to pass up serious concerns and known problems from engineers through the chain of command to the organization's top decision makers. Those midlevel managers actively discouraged safety-driven conversations. Engineers were then disciplined for "breaking ranks" when they attempted to "go around" their immediate supervisors to communicate with leaders who were higher up. Talking openly about even life-threatening safety concerns was treated as outright insubordination. Engineers' careers at NASA required their silence. NASA made it completely unsafe for people to speak freely.

In the end, top decision makers who made the ultimate "go" or "no go" call for launch and reentry had no information about the ultimately fatal concerns NASA's own engineers tried to communicate. Sadly, it took two major disasters for NASA to abandon its shoot-the-messenger approach. Its leaders reached the conclusion that the organization must once again return to a norm wherein anybody can talk to anybody at any time about safety concerns. To ensure openness and timely disclosure, channels of communication must be decoupled from the top-down authority structure. These disasters showed that no employee, regardless of rank, should require special permission to talk about life-threatening scenarios. It should always be safe to speak up.

To ensure openness and timely disclosure, channels of communication must be decoupled from the top-down authority structure.

Although the problems at NASA are obvious in retrospect, research shows that employees at ordinary workplaces are hesitant to talk openly about even mundane concerns they notice. Most often, they don't speak up for these key reasons:[22]

- Fear of retaliation
- Fear of being labeled a "troublemaker"
- Fear of damaging their relationship with their supervisor
- Fear of creating negative impacts for others

Leaders need to make every effort to make it safe to speak up. Followers must feel a sense of confidence that the team and supervisor will not embarrass, reject, or punish someone for speaking up. Followers must experience mutual respect and trust among team members and their supervisor. This can be accomplished with four major communication strategies.

Strategy 1: Communicate an Obligation to Talk

First, you need to disrupt the psychological contract that many followers assume: leaders are expected to issue orders and people simply follow those orders.[23] Respected organizational researcher Karl Weick showed that the necessity to talk should be part of all job descriptions.[24] Speak to your team about their responsibility to disclose and talk openly to identify and solve problems more effectively. Share what it means by encouraging every member of your organization to do the following:

- Freely offer important information without making others "dig" for it.
- Take the initiative to talk sooner rather than later.
- Share more information rather than less.

You can lead by example by disclosing potential issues regularly and setting the expectation for everyone to do the same.

Strategy 2: Provide a Motivating Rationale

People are more likely to disclose and speak up if they are given good reasons, a rationale for doing so. In many organizations, for example, new "gear" appears like magic with little explanation. Leaders do not always slow down to explain the purposes or reasons for new technologies and computer systems. For this reason, people are often slow to adopt and use potentially helpful innovations because they don't know why they should.

In one study exploring this tension, researchers found that nurses were more likely to speak up when they were given hands-on reasons to adopt new technologies and systems.[25] When surgeons took the time to explain the reasons for and importance of using the new technology, such as "it will help speed up patients' recovery time," the nurses who worked for those surgeons asked more questions than usual, spoke up about the new technology, and ultimately adopted its effective use more quickly. In contrast, when surgeons did not give any reasons for using the new technology, the nurses who worked directly with those surgeons did not believe the technology changes were important and did not speak up or ask questions about potential issues or their use and adoption.

The key behavior that made the difference is simple. It involves providing a rationale and a context for change. You can do this easily by giving your team clear reasons to speak up.

Strategy 3: Reduce the Risks of Speaking Up

You can take concrete steps to reduce the perceived risks of speaking up. In another hospital study, researchers James Detert and Ethan Burris studied the way effective surgeons encouraged more open communication and created ease in operating rooms by reducing the perceived power differences between themselves and the rest of the operating team.[26] Specifically, surgeons, the leaders in the room, did the following:

- They made it a point to take action when members of the surgical team offered input.
- They communicated explicitly that other members of the team were just as important as the surgeon.
- They communicated a sense of humility by mentioning their own limitations or shortcomings.
- They underreacted, rather than overreacted, when a team member made an error.

When the surgeons practiced these four behaviors, they reduced the perceived power distance between themselves and the rest of the team. By reducing the perceived difference in authority, they reduced the risks of speaking up.

Strategy 4: Reward People for Disclosing

Speaking up about problems requires an enormous amount of courage. It's important to create a culture that rewards this action. In hospitals, for instance, a mistake called *wrong-site surgery* is more common than the public realizes. Wrong-site surgery happens when a surgeon operates on the wrong part of a patient's body (e.g., on the left shoulder instead of the right shoulder) or does the wrong surgery entirely. A mistake like this happened at

Massachusetts General Hospital when Dr. David Ring incorrectly performed a surgery to alleviate carpal tunnel syndrome but the patient, "Marie," was really suffering from "trigger finger."[27]

Instead of hiding his mistake, Dr. Ring visited Marie in her recovery room as soon as he discovered he had made the error, within minutes of completing the procedure. Instead of talking to hospital administrators or attorneys, he went straight to Marie's recovery room. He explained his mistake, admitted that it was his fault, apologized, and then performed the correct surgery later the same day.

Dr. Ring then published his experience in the *New England Journal of Medicine*. In the case study, Dr. Ring took full responsibility for the error and detailed the various steps that he missed and the obstacles the surgical team experienced that made the mistake more likely. He explained numerous errors and complications. While this was potentially embarrassing, Dr. Ring explained why he published the case: "We hope to encourage health care practitioners to discuss such events, investigate them fully, disclose them quickly and clearly to . . . use these as learning opportunities and reduce risk for future patients."[28] Disclosing his mistakes did not hurt Dr. Ring's career at all. In fact, the medical community praised him in public forums and other articles for his courage for speaking transparently about his case. He was even soon promoted to the chief of his department and continued to have a celebrated career as a surgeon.

Things could have gone differently for Dr. Ring. Many hospitals might have punished him in a variety of ways for his disclosure. Fortunately, his leaders and peers at Massachusetts General Hospital had the good sense to let Dr. Ring flourish. The rewards he experienced for disclosing no doubt encouraged others to do the same. While Dr. Ring's rewards were rather dramatic, rewards in most workplace settings could start simply with explicit praise and increase accordingly from there.

LEVEL 4: PUT IT INTO PRACTICE

Let's make this even more practical. As a leader, what are some concrete ways to begin disclosing? Following is a boiled down list of what we have discussed and how you can implement such changes right away. Circle the takeaways that you would find most helpful for you.

Level 1: The Power of Disclosing

You can disclose in numerous ways. In the workplace, the following take-aways will get you started on the right foot.

- **Share your story.** Sharing your story is a powerful way to let yourself be known. Find appropriate ways to tell people about your background and life. It may seem counterintuitive, but sharing your weaknesses or "foibles" builds positive connections.
- **Reveal your emotions and thoughts authentically.** Your authenticity can be a source of strength. Your vulnerability will help people understand the real you and build bridges. Your authenticity creates space for others to do the same.
- **Communicate expectations.** We often assume that people already understand or sense what we want from them. But expectations are not common sense. It's best to explain your expectations openly and supportively, especially at the beginning of a leader-follower relationship. When followers know what you expect of them, they are much more likely to hit the target.
- **Express your gratitude.** Gratitude starts by identifying what you are thankful for in others and then taking the time to state it directly. Set aside a few quiet moments each week to reflect on, take notes on, and then tell some specific individuals about what you are grateful for.

Level 2: Deepen and Reinforce Relationships

One major benefit of disclosure is that it deepens relationships. Even under less-than-ideal situations, disclosure is often exactly what's needed to strengthen our connections with others.

- **Break the ice with purpose.** When opening meetings, leaders have a ready-made moment to encourage disclosure, especially if you sense that people are struggling with isolation. We suggested using the highlight-hero-hardship icebreaker.
- **Clarify what you really want.** We often get caught up trying to outmaneuver others in difficult conversations. A much better approach is to pause and clarify what we really want. This intentional process of self-awareness will clarify what we want out of a situation. Ask yourself: "What

do I want in this situation? What do I want for others? What do I want for the relationship?" The answers will show you how to move forward.

- **Use the WINFY framework.** The WINFY prompt provides a way to start important conversations, particularly when you sense that you are not understanding or seeing eye to eye with a person with whom you work. Each person takes turns starting their statements with "What I need from you is _____." The other person listens and takes notes. If done authentically, this is a powerful way to help a relationship turn a corner.
- **Apologize when you've made a mistake.** A genuine apology is usually the first step in explicitly identifying an error, clearing the air, and making efforts to remove whatever relational baggage stands between you and other people.

Level 3: Make It Safe for Others to Speak Up

Inevitably, problems happen at work. People will disclose in proportion to how safe they feel when doing so. Leaders can take concrete steps to make it easier for people to disclose.

- **Communicate an obligation to talk.** Let your team members know that they have a responsibility to disclose. Make disclosure part of every job description. In part, this means identifying potential issues so they can be solved earlier in their development.
- **Provide a motivating rationale.** Give people good reasons to say what's on their mind. Give them a clear rationale for wanting their input. Virtually every change, decision, or project has reasons for existing and needs employees' participation to be successful. Explain those reasons.
- **Reduce the risks of speaking up.** The average employee is afraid to speak up. Leaders should reduce the risks of doing so by putting suggestions into practice, communicating the followers' importance to the team effort, demonstrating humility, and underreacting to errors as they come up. Demonstrate that no harm will come from speaking openly.
- **Reward disclosure.** It's equally important to reward disclosure when it occurs. This means thanking people for sharing and for having the courage to speak up. Never "shoot the messenger." Consider how rewarding this straightforward statement is and the positive impact it could have:

"Thank you for bringing the issue to my attention. You did the right thing. I'll be following up and handling this immediately."

CONCLUSION

Disclosure doesn't come naturally to many people, especially in the workplace. It feels riskier than some of the other positive communication practices in this book. We believe the benefits of disclosing, such as deeper relationships and improved team effectiveness, are well worth the effort to stretch yourself. In addition, workplace cultures today have developed to the point where the teams we lead expect a certain amount of openness from leaders. When we don't disclose, they will notice something is missing and often draw their own conclusions.

Hollie Packman is an executive coach. She relayed a story recently about a chief human resources officer she once coached. Hollie explained, "She was known for her competence but also was seen as too 'buttoned-up' and formal. She was very careful to maintain her professional distance from subordinates, peers, and supervisors. She was so reserved that people began to question her thinking. They'd ask, 'Does she even have a perspective on this?' The feedback from her colleagues was that she needed to share her perspective, build relationships, and bring people along in the conversation more openly."

Hollie continued, "In this company, like many others, interpersonal distance is a trust killer. To turn things around, we worked on declaring or disclosing her intent. She started to explain her thinking to her colleagues, 'Here's why I'm doing what I'm doing.' She started to share details about what she was doing on the weekends and talking more openly about her interest and what she likes to do. She even started being open about issues like when she wasn't feeling well."

Hollie cast the issue of disclosure in a broader light. "I have executive clients who are going through chemo, they have sick children, they are going through a divorce. But they are not sharing anything about it with anybody. Meanwhile, other people are doing what people do. They are assigning meaning to behaviors. They think, 'She looks withdrawn. Oh, she's not interested,' Or, 'She's upset with me.' If there is something tragic happening, you absolutely need to share. You don't need to share all the details, just the headline. Like, 'There's something going on with my health.' That openness allows people to give you grace. Then, they won't judge you for being late to a meeting."

The benefits of disclosing, such as deeper relationships and improved team effectiveness, are well worth the effort to stretch yourself.

"Thankfully," Hollie concluded, "the executive I was working with made changes in becoming more known and more open. It made a big difference with how well she worked with her colleagues. Budgeting season came around not long after this and it had been a challenging year financially for the organization. Her improved connection with her colleagues allowed her to collaborate with people she would normally be competing with over money. Her increased vulnerability led to greater understanding from others which then led to more grace and trust from others." We encourage you to make the same shift. See box 5.6 to make your next steps even more concrete.

Positive leaders disclose to deepen relationships.

Box 5.6. **Top Takeaways**

Reflecting on your selections in the "Level 4: Put It into Practice" section, what are your top three takeaways?

1.

2.

3.

6

Encourage to Give Support

Imagine that we wanted to hire you to do a simple job for 12 hours per day. Your duties would be to fill burlap bags with sand. We'd give you a shovel, a pile of sand, and a bunch of empty bags. That's it. The work is tiring and dirty, but you'd get a few short breaks to eat. What hourly pay would you personally require to do that job?

Based on our training and teaching experience, people's answers vary, but the rate often starts with at least $30 per hour for college students and goes much higher among working professionals. Some participants say they would accept no less than $100 per hour for what they see as "pointless" and "mind-numbing" work. Many explain that they would only agree to do the job for a week or two.

Now, what if we told you *why* you're doing it? The reason you are filling bags of sand is to build a barrier and divert the rising floodwaters that are threatening a small town. This town is on the edge of a river that is overflowing because of record-breaking rainfall. About a dozen homes are in danger of being washed away. The people of this town need your help! You'd be working side by side with the families who live in these homes. Business owners, local fire and rescue workers, and community members would all be there right alongside you. They'd be offering their encouragement, gratitude, and appreciation for your hard work. They would be saying to you, "I can't tell you how much your help means to us. You're saving our town." Now, with this context in mind, what hourly pay would you accept to fill those bags with sand?

"He who has a why to live for can bear with almost any how."
—Friedrich Nietzsche

Once they know why they are doing the task, most people lower their price significantly. Many of them would even volunteer their time and do it for nothing. While the task itself didn't change, what changed is the purpose. As Friedrich Nietzsche said, "He who has a *why* to live for can bear with almost any *how*."[1]

This chapter focuses on the fifth proposition of the "Wheel of Positive Communication," which states: encourage to give your people the support they need to succeed. First, you'll learn the importance of encouraging your employees. Second, we will share positive communication strategies to give your employees more meaning at work. Third, you'll develop the skills and strategies to create a more compassionate workplace culture. Unlike complimenting, which is often focused on the present moment, encouraging others is an orientation toward the future.

LEVEL 1: THE POWER OF ENCOURAGING

Encouraging communication is powerful. For years, Julien has been telling students that they should learn to "ride the wave." Many of his students are at-risk or first-generation students. As they come closer to success, many panic. Julien tells them, "Relax a little bit, you're on the surfboard now. All you have to do is let the wave take you to success. You don't have to do anything special. All you need to do is ride the wave because you deserve it and have earned it."

Well, a few years ago Julien was not feeling so grounded himself. He had agreed to serve as chair of a department on campus where hostility and toxicity were present. The task was straightforward: to bring the faculty and staff of the department back together and recreate a positive space to work. Doing the job, however, was difficult. Julien would come home at night and talk about it to his wife. "How am I going to solve this riddle?" he would ask. "How am I going to bring people together?"

One morning he went to his office, opened his computer, and found an email from his wife. He was surprised because they don't typically communicate through his work email. He opened the message and in big bold letters, the email read: "RIDE THE WAVE!" Right underneath the message was a giant picture of a surfer in the heart of a wave. His wife had pasted an edited photo of Julien's smiling face onto the surfer. The thought, effort, and care in his wife's gesture gave Julien all of the encouragement he needed to face the challenges of the day ahead.

Positive communication for leaders is about learning to create moments like these. It is about learning to transform what may seem like ordinary moments into extraordinary ones—moments in which people truly feel affected by your words, your actions, and ultimately your support. So the question becomes, how can you do it? And why is it so important?

Leaders can transform what may seem like ordinary moments into extraordinary moments.

Recall our discussion from chapter 4 about the importance of employee engagement. One of the key questions on the twelve-question employee engagement survey is this: "Is there someone at work who encourages your development?" In other words, one of the key elements of being able to affect employees' engagement in a positive way is for them to feel encouraged and supported.

We've seen a common theme across organizations for many years now. In organizations that are struggling, employees report low levels of engagement, low levels of satisfaction, low morale, and unhappiness. As one participant said at a recent client workshop: "We need more happiness in our work. The morale is down, people don't trust one another, and there is confusion." Another person said: "We need to learn to operate as a team in a respectful professional environment. Thoughts and opinions are dismissed [here] and there is always a change that leads to more and more confusion. You may be told the 'why' but your opinion does not matter. They pretend to listen but it must be done their way no matter what."

Often, when people express these concerns, it is because they do not feel valued and supported. As researchers have shown, "Employees who perceive that their organization values their contributions, meets their socio-emotional needs, cares about their well-being and judges their jobs more favorably, report reduced stress, increased job satisfaction, as well as reduced turnover."[2] Given those needs, how can you help your people to weather hard times, welcome change in the company, and create an environment in which people will support one another?

Leaders need to encourage others. Stated simply, encouraging means "to give courage" and to help others in times of difficulty and challenge. It is the ability to use communication to give support, confidence, or hope. Encouraging is part of the larger purpose of giving social support. In the workplace, scholars define social support as "social relationships that integrate employees together to expand their capability for being buffered against stress."[3] Support, of course, can come from coworkers, but the most influential factor is the support that comes from the leader. When employees feel valued for their contributions and that their well-being is important to the leader, they experience reduced stress, increased job satisfaction, and better performance. In fact, the quality of management leadership explains 75 percent of the variance in social support.[4] In other words, leadership is the determining factor in shaping employees' experience. See box 6.1 to discover if your employees see you as an encouraging leader.

Positive leaders consistently communicate that teamwork is a number one priority, consult with their employees if decisions will affect their work, support them through a difficult task, remind each individual of their strengths when they face challenges, and express their confidence. These actions matter and cumulatively create a workplace where people feel supported. There are three keys to encouraging your employees. First, you can encourage by sharing information and giving meaningful advice. Second, you can encourage by alleviating distress and providing emotional support. Third, you can be encouraging by reminding your employees of the strengths they possess.

Key 1: Share Encouraging Information and Advice Relationally

An easy way to support people is by sharing the information they need to succeed. In one study, scholars collected daily written diaries of people across multiple organizations to see what leadership behaviors had the most impact on team morale and perceived quality of leadership.[5] The most important category was providing support. One key way effective leaders provide support to their teams is by sharing relevant information, especially during po-

Box 6.1. Do Your Employees See You as Encouraging?

Instructions: Take a moment to consider how your own employees might answer these statements about you. 1 represents strong disagreement and 5 represents strong agreement.[1]

My supervisor encourages their employees to work as a team.

1   2   3   4   5

My supervisor asks for my opinion before making decisions that affect my work.

1   2   3   4   5

My supervisor can be counted on to help me with a difficult task at work.

1   2   3   4   5

My supervisor reminds me of my strengths when I am discouraged about a task.

1   2   3   4   5

My supervisor expresses confidence in my ability to overcome difficulties.

1   2   3   4   5

What do your scores reveal? Each of these items says something important about how you can be a source of encouragement for your employees.

Note

1. Biganeh, M., & Young, S. L. (2021). Followers' perceptions of positive communication practices in leadership: What matters and surprisingly what does not. *International Journal of Business Communication.* https://doi.org/10.1177%2F2329488420987277

tentially stressful situations. Here is an example from a team member about a moment in which they felt supported. This is what they wrote in their diary:

> Jake called to pass along news of a pending organization change which has more positive implications than most of the rumors. I appreciated his call from [his] vacation to let me know of this glimmer of bright light in the sea of uncertainty.

The team member was referring to a brief moment, but the impact was huge. His manager made a phone call in the middle of his vacation to connect and share helpful information to reduce uncertainty. Here is another example from the study:

> Our project manager sat down with us and took time to share how she was feeling. It was fun, and it made me feel better to think that she trusted us with her feelings. This made me want to work harder so that I'd be more supportive of her and the team. It also made me feel lucky to be part of a team where others can take time to share honestly.

In both stories the act of disclosure led to the experience of feeling supported. Sharing helpful information reduced the team members' uncertainty and encouraged them to overcome difficulties.

In addition to sharing helpful information, numerous opportunities exist to share encouraging advice. When people recall memorable messages in their lives, most of those messages are actually advice that they have received from leadership figures. Memorable messages typically only have two required elements: they can easily be brought back to mind over the long run, and they had a big impact on people.

For Julien, a memorable message from his supervisor helped him stop a bad habit. For years, Julien had been thinking about quitting smoking but was not able to make it happen. One day Rob, Julien's supervisor at the time, joined him at Burger King for a quick lunch. Out of nowhere, Rob gave Julien some advice. He said: "You know how you quit smoking, don't you? You just do it one cigarette at a time." It's hard to explain how or why this statement clicked for Julien. He didn't quit right away, but a few weeks later the opportunity came. Instead of waking up and having his first cigarette as he usually would, he took a shower instead. When he realized that he had skipped the first cigarette, he remembered Rob's advice. He thought, "If I can skip this cigarette, I can skip the next one." Julien never smoked again.

Advice giving is a powerful form of encouragement, especially in the early stages of one's career or early on in a new position. As a leader, you can draw on your life experience, share meaningful stories with your employees, and give real and tangible advice to your team. Explore box 6.2 for some suggestions, realizing that drawing on your personal experience is best.

The impact of the advice can also expand beyond the moment. For example, in a study conducted by communication scholar Cynthia Stohl, one participant received this feedback from her boss while she was at her desk after completing her tasks: "If you're not helping, you're hindering."[6] In

---

Box 6.2. **Down to Earth Advice Will Have an Impact**

Often even ordinary sounding advice can provide volumes of encouragement. Consider the following examples:

- ✓ "Don't listen to the noise. Just keep doing the work in front of you and you'll come out on top of this."
- ✓ "This is a temporary setback. Your career is still moving forward."
- ✓ "Remember, this is a marathon, not a sprint. Pace yourself."
- ✓ "Sometimes we need to accept that we did the best we could, learn from the experience, and keep going."

Out of context, statements like these might sound ordinary. But when said by the right person, at the right moment, in the right situation, advice like this can move the mountains inside us.

---

reflecting on the experience, she said he had shared the message "with the intent to get me to help the others out that day, but I realized that it really was the way I was supposed to act all the time. Now, I'm always checking to see how I can help, what we do is so important!" After analyzing hundreds of memorable messages in the workplace, Stohl showed that advice giving is beneficial to employees and the mission of the organization. First, she said, "memorable messages provide a guide to behavior appropriate for the organizational setting." Second, they create a shared understanding of the workplace and what is valued.

Positive leaders share helpful information and advice to encourage their employees. This is a fundamental way of providing support to the people you work with. Doing so will foster your employees' learning, increase their job competency, create belonging, and increase resiliency.

Key 2: Alleviate Distress by Providing Support

There are many ways of showing emotional support, but the energy that drives it is empathy, the ability to imagine how others feel and respond to their hardships and suffering. In a study we mentioned earlier in which researchers collected daily diaries from team members across multiple organizations, the authors found that two behaviors are key when providing emotional support.

First, great leaders alleviate stressful situations for subordinates. They act on the information they have and take the initiative to problem solve. In doing so, they help alleviate stressful situations. Here is an example from an employee's diary:[7]

> The one event that happened today that surprised and really made me feel good was that, on Monday, I shared with Ming [business team manager] that I was disappointed in the fact that several of our team members have been waiting for me to monitor when something was due from them, and then they scramble around trying to get things done the last minute. I gave him a written list of examples on projects that were time constrained. He asked me if I would be available for a meeting this afternoon, and of course I responded positively. Imagine my surprise when I went in and he had everybody that owed a response/action sitting around a conference table for a work session where they would give a date that they would complete all their projects and get us back up to date! You could not ask for more from a business team manager—he is a terrific leader! And best of all, we were able to all do it without any hard feelings.

Second, the best supervisors create opportunities to listen to subordinates' negative feelings. We have often observed that the shortest road between a leader and follower is empathy. You don't need to have the skills of a professional therapist to check in, ask people how they are doing, and listen well. Consider this story taken from another employee's diary.[8]

> This morning my project manager came over and sat next to me and asked me if I was okay after all the firing that went on yesterday. I thought that was really nice since we all had a very rough day yesterday. . . . I'm now trying to concentrate on what IS in my control [by] doing my job.

In short, you can alleviate distress by showing your employees that you are present, you understand, and you care. Many people struggle with empathy, but anybody can improve with effort and practice. As Maya Angelou said, "I think we all have empathy. We may not have enough courage to display it."[9] When you consistently show your people you care, you will create a supportive environment for all.

The shortest road between a leader and a follower is empathy.

Key 3: Refocus on Strengths

You can also encourage others by refocusing them on their strengths. This is especially important when people are beating themselves up the way Anneliese was doing recently. The camera was fixed on Anneliese and we were ready for our interview. The focus of the interview was part of a large project with adults from all walks of life in which we ask them to recount a "peak" conversation, a conversation that gave them a great sense of happiness and joy at work.[10]

"I remember being really panicked," Anneliese recalled. "So, I called someone who's higher up in the district." She was bawling as she dialed the number. "I've messed up," she said right away on the phone. "What do I do? How do I fix it?"

As she told her story, she skipped most of the discussion. What stuck with her most is what her supervisor said at the end of the conversation. "I remember her saying this to me," Anneliese recalled. "You're really good at what you do. You are good at your job and you care."

"Those words," Anneliese reflected, "have really stuck with me. And even though I'm not in that position anymore, I've carried it to my next job."

This leader refocused Anneliese on her strengths, a form of esteem support. Esteem support includes any messages that are designed to enhance how people feel about themselves that strengthen another person's understanding of who they are and what they can do.[11] As shown in Anneliese's story, the leader's message affected the way she saw herself in the moment, but it also improved how she saw herself in the future. This advice resonates with what Abraham Maslow once wrote: "People are both actuality and potentiality."[12] Anneliese later reported, "I learned that challenges happen, but you can always overcome them. I learned that I do care about what I do and to always take pride in my work and I have become more confident in my work. I'm not scared of challenges anymore." Esteem support is powerful because it occurs after a person has experienced a threat to their self-esteem. It helps the person realign how they see themselves, who they are, what their skills are, and what they can accomplish.

As a positive leader, you need to find ways of helping your employees refocus on their strengths, especially after setbacks, challenges, or failures. These are key moments in which you may sound more like a coach than a typical supervisor. In one study exploring athletes' most memorable messages from high school coaches, researchers Gregory Cranmer, Christine Anzur, and

Michael Sollitto found three types of esteem support messages you can add to your leadership style.[13]

One form of esteem support is to emphasize people's capabilities to succeed. This can be done by recognizing past performance or expressing potential for future performance. Here are some examples of messages you might use in your approach:

- "You are capable of doing this. You can be a better leader than that."
- "You have all the skills you need to succeed with this project; I know you will hit it out of the park."

A second way is to recognize the qualities of the person by focusing on their strengths and reminding them to tap into their concentration, their focus, and their effort. Coaches shared many messages about how to do this with their athletes, but here are some to use in the context of leadership:

- "Just go slowly and steadily on this one. This is a five-year innovative project you are working on. You are only going to get stronger."
- "You are an innovative leader. Find a way to inspire your team to finish this quarter with some punch."

A third way is to reinforce the relationships between people on the team. Often this is done by reminding athletes that they serve a critical role for the team and are connected to others. One coach, for example, told one athlete, "We are a team. We work together and we finish as a whole." Another coach said, "It is important to stick together as a team and support each other." But the most critical form of building esteem is to remind the individual that they are an inspiration to others. For example, you might say to one of your seasoned employees, "You are a role model for our new hires. You are one of the best leaders we have ever had."

Encouragement is at the heart of leading others positively.

Once you have a handle on skills such as sharing ideas and advice, alleviating stress, and refocusing the conversation on other's strengths, it's time to level up your skills and give your employees a "why" they can work for.

LEVEL 2: GIVE WORK MORE MEANING

Leaders play a pivotal role in giving meaning to their followers' work. It's incredibly motivating to understand the larger significance of our day-to-day tasks. You can support your team's efforts with four habits.

Habit 1: Talk (a Lot) about the Big Picture

Employees often focus on the trees but can't see the whole forest. This leaves many people dissatisfied and disconnected from the ultimate value or meaning of the work. Often privately, people stew with emotion, "Does my work even matter? Am I making an impact?" One practical way to answer these questions is to talk about the big picture and express the long-term impact people's work will have and to remind people *why* their work matters.

Years ago, Alex did an internship at a small management consulting firm based in Los Angeles where he worked with Allen Weiner. We mentioned Allen in a previous chapter. As part of his role, Alex helped prepare 360-feedback reports on hundreds of high-level executives across numerous Fortune 500 companies. Looking at these reports, Alex found a key skill that was consistently ranked lowest in the quantitative data among virtually all executives: the leaders showed an inability to communicate "a broad strategic view of the business." Years' worth of data on hundreds of executives showed the same tendency. The qualitative feedback about these leaders regularly indicated, for example, "[X leader] doesn't tell us what this is all about. He only tells me what to do." In other words, most leaders received high marks on talking about the details of their team's daily work, but few leaders excelled at articulating how that work contributed to the big-picture vision and long-term purpose.

In a recent conversation with Allen, the consulting firm's founder, he explained the various ways he would coach these leaders. "The problem," Allen explained, "is that leaders like these are stuck in 'the weeds,' in the minute details of issues." Focusing too much on the details can make both leaders and followers lose sight of *why* they are doing the work, the meaningful contribution their work makes to the overall goal. Allen said, "I'd normally start these coaching conversations by telling the executives, 'I think you have [a big-picture perspective], I just don't think you talk about it.'" He would then coach his clients to talk deliberately about the big-picture context of the team's work (see box 6.3 for concrete examples you can draw on). He coached executives to take the time to add a talking point about the big picture to any upcoming presentations, team updates, or important conversations.

> ## Box 6.3. How to Talk about the "Big Picture"
>
> Allen Weiner suggests leaders add talking points to most messages that focus on the team's big picture. Here are some sample starter sentences that can easily be used in any conversation or presentation to do just that:
>
> - ✓ "Let's not forget what this is all about . . ."
> - ✓ "Let's be sure not to take our eyes off the prize, to be as competitive as possible with company x and y."
> - ✓ "I think when we look back on this a year from now, we're going to see x, y, z. That's my vision for what we're doing."
>
> Adding talking points like these prompts executives to first think about the big picture for their own benefit and then talk about it for the team's benefit.

Explaining the team's purpose, vision, and long-term goals occasionally doesn't cut it. Leaders can and should continually explain the deeper meaning of followers' work by spelling out the difference their accomplishments make and the value they add. Allen continued, "It's a little bit like the difference between explaining the features and benefits of a product or service. When we focus on features, those are the details and specs that a given product includes. That puts us back in 'the weeds.' Who cares? What does it matter? What do those features and specs do for you? As customers, we want to know the benefits, the value of those features. The same is true for followers. Leaders need to remind followers of the long-term, big-picture benefits, contribution, and value of their work." Conversations like these instantly provide more meaning to and encouragement for followers' work.

Habit 2: Share the Context and Provide Perspective

Similarly, leaders can also give followers more meaning and encouragement by providing needed context and perspective. If nothing else, the

COVID-19 pandemic revealed that employees need reassurance and reminders about what really counts. People regularly look at their ever-changing professional landscape and ask themselves, "What does this change mean for me? How will this influence my life? Will I still have this job a year from now? Do I still even want this job?" Postpandemic, these questions are just as relevant. Left to fend for themselves, many people imagine anxiety-inducing worst-case scenarios, especially during times of uncertainty. Leaders can offer better answers that encourage and support followers' efforts to reduce their uncertainty. This can easily be done by sharing the context behind decisions and goals and providing the perspective employees need to see the future.

To do so, you need to scan the environment for information, notice relevant changes, and put all of that "data" into context for followers. Use communication to actively reduce uncertainty. This can be done in at least three ways. Check the box next to any of the following leadership behaviors you do when your team is facing uncertainty:

☐ **Acknowledge organizational challenges transparently.**
Openly discussing difficulties is more productive than pretending emerging issues don't exist or don't matter. When things get messy at work, identify the issues clearly and start a discussion.

☐ **Remind followers of the team's highest, unchanging priorities.**
This is about grounding followers. When it seems like the world is spinning out of control, reassure your team by reminding them about the foundational, enduring, and nonnegotiable parts of the team's purpose and vision.

☐ **Chart a course.**
When the best course of action isn't yet obvious, many of us freeze in place. We're not sure what to do. Instead, leaders can have an immediate impact by pointing followers in the right direction, even before the dust settles. In the game of chess and in many other arenas, there's an old expression, "A bad plan is better than no plan." Even if plans change, taking some thoughtful initiative will spark followers into action.

Practices like these begin to clarify an otherwise blurry world of work. We expand on this conversation later in the chapter when we talk about more serious situations like crises.

Habit 3: Help Your Employees Develop a Personal Vision

Positive leaders can give meaning to followers by helping them develop a personal vision for their careers. In professional circles, we often hear about mission and vision statements for organizations. We hear less about crafting a vision or roadmap for people's individual careers. In fact, we may be hesitant to speak openly about "where we'd like to be in five years," because goals like that may not always include our current employer. Still, leaders only help themselves when they help their followers see the possibilities for their own long-term careers.

We mentioned Rob Ulmer earlier. He was our chair when we both were first hired for our teaching careers. Among other strengths, Rob has a gift of turning seemingly ordinary events into memorable moments that contributed to a personal vision for our careers. For instance, any time Julien, Alex, or other young faculty members received news that one of our journal articles was accepted for publication, Rob would make a big deal out of it. Instead of just giving us a verbal pat on the back, Rob would say, "Let's get lunch today and talk about it." We'd then celebrate the accomplishment over a meal. He'd talk about how the publication would make a difference and build our credibility in our respective areas of expertise and how each published article, chapter, or book was building a long-term body of work that we would have with us for the rest of our careers. Similarly, when articles were rejected or when we experienced professional setbacks, Rob helped us see those moments with the long-term view in mind. His approach contrasts sharply with the competitive sink-or-swim approach to publishing experienced in many academic departments.

By celebrating our successes and making these moments more memorable, Rob was also casting a vision for our career trajectories as young faculty. In one-on-one meetings, he would regularly put each young faculty member's teaching success and publications into context. He'd show how our hard work was positioning us for future promotions and careers that were full of promise. He'd explain the types of longer-term professional opportunities he saw for us that would come from our present-day efforts. Rob forecast how our influence would grow from individual contributors to influential leaders in the field. Many years later, we remember our conversations with Rob clearly. He helped give meaning to moments that otherwise might have passed by without much notice.

Leaders can help cast a powerful professional vision
for each individual on the team.

Interestingly, very little time in these conversations focused on what he as the chair of the department needed from us or the results the college expected. These conversations never felt strategic or managerial. Rob seldom talked about what the department needed from faculty. Virtually everything in these conversations sincerely celebrated our accomplishments along the way and cast a vision for how young teachers like us were building our long-term professional lives. Though each of these conversations was uniquely tailored to each young faculty member, we all experienced similar benefits. His words reduced the uncertainty and anxiety that many new faculty members feel in their first few years on the job and provided us with a personal vision and road map for our early careers. These conversations helped us look beyond the day to day "grind" of seemingly endless hard work and to vividly picture the future we were building.

Habit 4: Create Meaningful Turning Points

Leaders can also shape their workplace cultures in positive ways by taking advantage of the typical rites of passage followers go through. Most of us are familiar with major rites of passage like a promotion or new job title. Many formal moments like this exist, especially early in our employment such as moving from a part-time, "casual," or seasonal position to a full-time or permanent position that comes with a salary and benefits package. Some leaders and colleagues pause to offer their congratulations or mark moments like these. A leader's thoughtful words of encouragement and support in these moments deepen the significance of the occasion. A leader, in other words, can make these moments feel even more "official." Using box 6.4, take a moment to reflect about what you are currently doing to welcome new employees.

Our career trajectories are also filled with an endless string of "firsts." You receive your first paycheck, give your first presentation, lead your first meeting, meet your first big client, or participate in your first off-site retreat or conference with the rest of the team. Some of these moments happen out in the open, but many of these micro-events pass without external acknowledgment. As leaders, these are all opportunities to celebrate the progress each

Box 6.4. **What Informal Rites of Passage Do You Celebrate?**

Instructions: Consider the various informal rites of passage newly hired professionals experience. Put a check mark next to each item you currently do to welcome new hires.

- ☐ You introduce them to the rest of the team individually.
- ☐ You give them a key to the building.
- ☐ You make sure a nameplate is added to their office door.
- ☐ You make sure their business cards are ordered on their first day of employment.
- ☐ You add their photo to the website as soon as possible.

In addition to these items, what other opportunities do you have to create meaningful turning points out of informal interactions that might otherwise just pass by with little notice?

person is making. Leaders can make each of these moments more encouraging, supportive, and filled with meaning by taking the time to say just a few words, such as, "Well, team, I'd just like to pause and acknowledge that Mark did his first client presentation yesterday. Great job, Mark."

By adding your leadership touch to emphasize multiple rites of passage like these, you can create meaningful turning points for the members of your team. These turning points can increase followers' connection and commitment.

Several years ago, Alex's wife, Erin, started diving again in her forties and joined a diving club in the community. The typical age range for her fellow divers is eight to eighteen, so Erin was the only adult diver on the team and often felt out of place. She also noticed that her coach gave fun nicknames to virtually all of the young divers after a couple of seasons on the team. Often, each nickname was well thought-out to ensure each one was a custom fit. During diving practice, the coach called out these nicknames over a megaphone to provide feedback, "Great back dive, Vitamin-C!" After almost two years on the team, however, Alex's wife had still not received her nickname. As the only adult diver, she began to wonder if her coach would ever give her one. Then one day, she returned home from practice and said, "I got my nickname today!" "What is it?" Alex asked. "Colorado!" she beamed with pride. Her face lit up and illustrated that she'd experienced a turning point on the team. She reported, "He said, 'Excellent pike, Colorado.'" As illustrated in this story, leaders should not underestimate the value of creating deliberate turning points as ways to support, encourage, and give more meaning to followers' experiences.

In addition to these four habits, leaders can also integrate encouragement into the cultural fabric of the entire organization. That's the third level of performance we hope you will embrace.

LEVEL 3: CREATE A CULTURE OF SUPPORT

Today, many leaders are asking themselves timely questions. "How can I create a supportive environment for all?" "What initiatives and strategies will help foster a positive workplace environment?" According to an article by Jason Kanov and his research team, "Employee grief costs U.S. businesses about $75 billion annually, while job stress and burnout have been estimated to cost industry hundreds of billions of dollars annually."[14] In this section, we show you three ways to create a culture of support across your organizations. First, you'll learn how to build a compassionate workplace. Then, we focus on organizational resilience. Finally, you'll learn a proven approach to lead your team through a crisis.

Strategy 1: Build Compassion into Your Team's DNA

When things get difficult, we all benefit from a little compassion. When leaders demonstrate a preference for compassion, their followers are 25 percent more engaged in their jobs, 20 percent more committed, and at an 11 percent lower risk of burnout.[15] Leaders also benefit directly. When they show compassion, they experience a 30 percent increase in their sense of well-being and happiness in their lives. Receiving compassion can be a powerful source of encouragement.[16]

Jane Dutton, professor emerita at the University of Michigan's Ross School of Business, recently wrote: "Organizations are often faced with situations in which their members suffer."[17] These might include natural disasters such as floods, earthquakes, or hurricanes; human-made disasters such as accidents or errors; and personal tragedies including death, illness, and divorce. There are also everyday job stressors such as layoffs, restructuring, or personal injuries. Dutton and her colleagues then noted, "While organizations have the opportunity to respond to this pain, not all do so, nor do it well."[18]

By analyzing case studies and organizations that respond particularly well to pain and suffering, Dutton and her colleagues developed an approach called "Compassion Organizing"—a phrase used to describe the productive process that occurs when "individuals in organizations notice, feel, and respond to human pain in a coordinated way."[19] Focus on the key words here; compassion occurs when people do the following:

√ *Notice* the pain and suffering that is taking place around them.
√ *Feel* the pain and suffering that others are experiencing.
√ And more importantly, *respond* together.

In other words, the term "compassion" is not simply a knee-jerk emotion or a feeling, but instead refers to an organization's ability to *respond* to the pain and suffering of others. As the authors explained, "Compassion organizing creates a pattern of collective action that represents a distinct form of organizational capability that alleviates pain by extracting, generating, coordinating, and calibrating resources to direct toward those who are suffering."[20]

When organizations respond with compassion to individual- or group-level pain and suffering, they can embrace numerous benefits. Compassion helps people feel acknowledged by the organization, promotes faster recovery, and reveals that the organization cares about them and values their well-being, which in turn improves employee satisfaction and performance. A secondary benefit is related to the people across the organization who are part of the compassionate response. Compassion elevates us and creates positive emotions and experiences for those who are providing the support. Finally, "engaging in compassion at work has implications for how connected individuals feel to their organization, work colleagues, and ultimately to key organizational outcomes . . . heightened connection to others culminates in a greater commitment to one's organization, with well-established implications for important organizational outcomes such as lower levels of turnover."[21] In box 6.5, you'll see the basic elements of a compassionate leadership response.

Leaders can make compassion one of the core values of the organization. We especially recommend the following three approaches to build it into your team's DNA.

Box 6.5. **How to Create a Culture of Compassion**

For leaders, personal engagement in the daily work of showing compassion will be key. This can be done simply with these three steps:

1. *Pay attention to your employees' experiences.*
   Become aware of the presence of suffering, whether it is at the
   individual or group level.
2. *Show your understanding and "suffer with" people by emotionally connecting with them.*
   Invite dialogue, ask for frank feedback, or collect data for large
   organizations to gauge how people are doing, especially during
   turbulent periods.
3. *Take actions to alleviate the suffering.*
   This is the most important part for leaders. Compassion is ultimately about responding. Leaders can respond by providing
   emotional support, giving material goods, organizing a response
   with a team or unit, granting time off or flexibility as needed, or
   launching a task force or initiative.

First, incorporate a lot of play time. Even as people grow up, playing
with others is actually at the heart of how we build empathy. As researchers
Celia Brownell, Stephanie Zerwas, and Geetha Balaraman wrote, "Play forces
children to behave altruistically and to take account of one another's feelings,
whether real or imagined."[22] This is still true of adults. Playing may include
ice breakers, team-building meetings, or impromptu games and competi-
tions, all of which can easily be incorporated throughout the week. When
Julien served as dean, for instance, for one full year he bought everyone a
toy popper for each person's birthday. Equipped with gentle foam balls, the
popper became a toy for the team to play with. Colleagues would "pop" by
the office, say "hi," and shoot a few poppers. Playtime connects us with the
humanity in each other and helps us see others in a different light. Playtime,
of course, needs to be balanced with a maintained focus on work. Compassionate organizations find the right balance.

Second, create an environment where people offer help to one another.
Remember that compassion is built on the notion of noticing how others are doing. Therefore, you need to establish a group expectation that
people should and will help one another. People can do this very simply by

volunteering or offering help when needed. Here is what one person said that illustrates our point well: "I know they're having a bad day, they've got all this work on their desk, and I'll go over and help them."[23]

Third, offer effective orientation and onboarding programs to new employees. One critical element of compassion is that people need to know and feel connected to one another. Orientations in organizations are a perfect place to do this. As researchers showed, you need to socialize "newcomers in the unit in ways that expose them to new tasks and people."[24] Today, over 70 percent of business leaders feel that effective onboarding is "an urgent and essential priority."[25] High-quality employee orientation and onboarding programs have been shown to effectively socialize newcomers and increase their knowledge and performance skills. Good orientation programs are also related to a wide variety of outcomes such as satisfaction, loyalty, and retention. Well-designed programs, researchers wrote, are actually "the most influential pieces of an employee's development."[26] These programs set up employees for success, connect people, and set the stage for compassion.

You can create a compassionate culture by placing these elements at the forefront of your organization, units, or division. Once you have created a compassionate environment, you are not only preparing for the present; you are laying the foundation for the future. When setbacks or disasters strike, you and your team will be ready to respond. The expectations for kindness and support will be clear.

Strategy 2: Respond to Crisis with a Focus on Renewal

Many workplaces feel as if they are in a constant state of flux and challenge. Leaders play a vital role in providing order in the midst of this complexity and building a resilient team that can respond to unexpected crises. The crisis could be a natural disaster, disease outbreaks, product failures, incidents of unethical leadership, or sabotage. News headlines show all too often that many leaders handle crises like these poorly and usually make the situation worse by blaming others, pointing fingers, or not sharing information. This type of response can sink a company. Fortunately, there are more positive and effective ways to respond to a crisis.

One inspiring approach is to respond with *renewal*. As researchers Robert Ulmer, Tim Sellnow, and Matt Seeger explained it, the renewal process communicates "a fresh sense of purpose and direction an organization discovers after it emerges from a crisis."[27] A driving force of renewal is the belief that most crises offer potential opportunities. Ulmer and his colleagues explained that in Mandarin, the word *crisis* combines two symbols: the one for *crisis* and the one for *opportunity*. In this spirit, it's up to the leader to bring those opportunities into clearer view. Approaching these challenges from the optimistic view of renewal is an example of positive leadership that can help teams grow and prosper and bounce back from crises more easily. Drawing on their work, you can turn any crisis into an opportunity by doing the following.[28]

Focus on the future. When a crisis occurs, leaders and teams often get stuck in a cycle of looking back even well after the actual crisis phase has passed. There is some value to looking back, but many organizations get bogged down in it. Renewing a team's focus involves sparking forward momentum to create the organization's future.

Alex was once a member of a church that was stuck looking back rather than forward. After attending services for a few months, he had already heard numerous references to the dramatic departure of a previous leader and the "church split." He heard about it in sermons from the pulpit and in casual conversations. People talked about the events as if these changes had happened recently. When Alex asked follow-up questions, however, he learned the previous leader had left the church more than five years earlier. Since that time, over 50 percent of the church's members were new. Most of the other new members had no firsthand memory of the previous leader or the crisis. These changes were fairly traumatic for many of the church's original members but meant almost nothing to new people. By continuing to dwell on those events, the church had trouble making forward progress. Thankfully, not long after this the leadership team changed their focus entirely and adopted a future-oriented view. They turned their attention from the past to the future. Over the next year or so, the mood in the church improved across the board. The leaders' renewed focus on the future made a big difference in finally renewing the culture and moving forward.

Crises can provide leaders the opportunity to look to the future and rejuvenate the team's mission and atmosphere.

Maintain a steady optimism. Unexpected changes often crush people's spirit and knock them down hard. Great leaders, however, don't have the luxury of staying down. They must pick themselves up. Leaders and their teams must look for the opportunities in the crisis to start fresh and build something new. It's part of the leader's role to focus on exciting possibilities, unexpected opportunities, and strengths that most changes expose. Changes and crises often reveal parts of a team's process that no longer work and create space for something new.

Choose honesty over strategy. When times get difficult, the best and most inspiring leaders adapt to the moment and speak from the heart. They even let their emotions show.

In 1995, Malden Mills, a textile mill in Massachusetts, experienced a horrible explosion and fire that drew national attention because of how the company's leader, Aaron Feuerstein, responded. He both demonstrated honesty over strategy and maintained a steady optimism. For decades the company was known for manufacturing its proprietary fabric, Polartec. The mill was also the community's largest employer. While the mill fire was still smoldering in the background, he announced his plan to rebuild the company and continuing paying employees their salaries even though they were out of work. Numerous board members disagreed with his approach, but Feuerstein ignored their advice. He spoke from the gut about how important Malden Mills was to its local community and how good the community had been to him personally over the years. He said in an interview at the time, "I'm not throwing 3,000 people out of work two weeks before Christmas."[29] His openness and vision inspired the community and industry to rally behind him. When they heard about his commitment, corporate clients like Patagonia and L.L. Bean even pledged to stick with Feuerstein instead of switching to other suppliers while he rebuilt the mill. The company's leadership clearly acknowledged the way the fire would set things back but also noted how the fire created the freedom and opportunity to buy new equipment, update the facilities, and create new methods and processes. Positive changes like these were all overdue. The leader used the fire to reinvigorate the team's conversation and culture with optimism.

Interpret events proactively. Unexpected changes, crises, and big failures are make-or-break leadership moments. Uncertainty, ambiguity, and confusion often peak during crises. Strong leaders don't wait for outsiders or naysayers to define a situation to suit their own agenda or allow confusion to dominate. Effective leaders are quick to speak up and take the initiative to become the primary interpreters and communicators of events. Unfortunately, this is difficult in large organizations. Rather than speaking quickly, it's more common to run every message by the public relations team or corporate lawyers for official approval. This usually results in leadership messages that are strategically crafted and watered down to avoid saying something wrong rather than saying what needs to be said. Messages like this sound calculated, empty, and sometimes simply rude. In contrast, great leaders are genuine, authentic, and in the moment. During uncertain times, followers crave leaders who speak immediately and from the heart. Take a moment now to check whether you are truly ready for crisis by taking our quick assessment in box 6.6.

Box 6.6. **Ready for Renewal?**

Instructions: Ryan Fuller and his colleagues developed an assessment tool to gauge how prepared organizations are to respond to crisis with renewal.[1] Use the following questions to evaluate your readiness to use crises as potential opportunities for renewal. Circle the answer below each question that best reflects your own leadership approach and team dynamics.

- In my organization, we embrace failure as an opportunity to learn.

  Strongly Disagree   Disagree   Not Sure   Agree   Strongly Agree

- Throughout a crisis event, my organization remains hopeful.

  Strongly Disagree   Disagree   Not Sure   Agree   Strongly Agree

- My organization views crises as turning points that have the potential for future positive outcomes.

  Strongly Disagree   Disagree   Not Sure   Agree   Strongly Agree

Were you able to agree or strongly agree with any of these questions? What do your answers reveal about your own leadership and your team's ability to respond to a crisis with a mindset of renewal? Rather than being stunned or looking backward, you can approach difficult situations by looking for unexpected opportunities and ways to spark renewal. Leaders who take this approach get things moving in the right direction sooner rather than later.

Note

1. Fuller, R. P., Ulmer, R. R., McNatt, A., & Ruiz, J. B. (2019). Extending discourse of renewal to preparedness: Construct and scale development of readiness for renewal. *Management Communication Quarterly, 33,* 272–301.

LEVEL 4: PUT IT INTO PRACTICE

Taken together, the suggestions in this chapter will equip any leader to encourage, give meaning, and create positive and supportive teams. Following are practical takeaways from the chapter. Circle the top takeaway in each area that you could see yourself putting into practice.

Employ the Power of Encouraging

- **Share helpful information and relational advice.** When done sincerely and with care, people will respond positively to good advice and helpful information. When your followers are struggling, guide them with encouragement and reassurance.
- **Alleviate distress.** Leaders can't solve all followers' problems and shouldn't try to. Still, you can come alongside them, "be there," and show you care when your team members are in distress. Leaders can listen to followers who are struggling, display empathy, and acknowledge the difficulties they are going through.
- **Refocus on strengths.** As a leader, you can help build followers' esteem by calling out their ability to succeed, naming their enduring positive qualities, and reinforcing the relationships among the team members. You can remind them of the strengths they already have.

Give Meaning to Followers' Efforts

- **Talk (a lot) about the big picture.** Rather than getting stuck "in the weeds," you can remind yourself and the team about the bigger vision and long-term goals their work is pursuing. Tell your followers about all the ways their efforts are contributing to something bigger than themselves.
- **Share the context and give perspective.** Use your past experiences to add context, perspective, and order to the conversation. When uncertainty, ambiguity, and anxiety increase, acknowledge the challenges the team faces, remind the team of its highest and unchanging priorities, and chart a course to move forward.
- **Help your employees develop a personal vision.** You can paint a vivid picture for each of your followers' professional development and career

path. Clarify how you see each follower's future playing out. Explain how you see followers' specific accomplishments as moving them closer to their desired professional futures.

- **Create meaningful turning points.** Use your team's existing formal and informal rites of passage to add more meaning to followers' progress. Pause, mark the occasion, and say a few words to elevate ordinary moments into more meaningful and memorable turning points.

Create a Culture of Support

- **Build compassion into your team's DNA.** One the one hand, compassion means noticing and responding to the various types of pain and suffering on or around your team. On the other hand, compassion means creating the type of environment where people offer help to their fellow team members.
- **Respond to crisis with a focus on renewal.** When crisis or unexpected events rock your team, don't get stuck looking back. Let the goal of renewing your team drive your communication. Communicate about the future, take an optimistic view, speak spontaneously and from the heart, and take an assertive role in interpreting what those changes will mean for the team.

CONCLUSION

Our chapter offers a simple principle: **when you choose to encourage, you are choosing to give meaning and support to your team.** As shown, you can and should offer encouragement at the individual level, at the team level, and across your organization. One of our colleagues who serves as a health-care performance consultant recently shared this fact in a conversation: "A staggering 94% of employees who quit say they would have stayed if their employers were interested in their development." To keep their most talented people, leaders must become more proactive in encouraging their people, stoking their passion, and giving them reasons for doing their jobs to the best possible extent.

You have it in you to create extraordinary moments for your people. As the illustration about filling bags with sand in the opening of the chapter showed, people really are willing to dig deep, go to great lengths to support others, and give more of themselves. As a leader, you have the capacity and the tools to encourage others, give more meaning to their work, and offer the support your followers need, especially when things get difficult. It's up to the leaders in the room to light the way. When you do, your people will rise to the occasion. See box 6.7 to make your plans to encourage others even more concrete.

Positive leaders encourage to give others the support they need.

Box 6.7. **Top Takeaways**

Reflect on your selections in the "Level 4: Put It into Practice" section. What are your top three takeaways?

1.

2.

3.

7

Listen to Transcend Differences

Melissa has worked in fundraising for twenty-five years. During a recent presentation, she shared a pivotal moment in her professional development. She recalled a conversation that took place right after visiting a donor and asking for a significant donation.

Given the size of the possible gift, she brought her boss with her to the appointment. Melissa said: "We had this great conversation to kick things off and then we jumped into business. The meeting lasted a little more than an hour." At the end of the meeting, "We were thanking her for her time and telling her how much we appreciate her." But Melissa did not feel good about the conversation at all.

She got back to the car, took a deep breath, and said to her boss: 'Well, I wish that could have gone a little better!'"

Melissa was frustrated with the result of the conversation. Her boss, however, saw it differently. He said: "I think the meeting went well. She's going to change how she pays the gift and we've got to provide her another option or two for a naming opportunity, but I think it went well. But you probably missed that because you talked too much.'"

"Holy smokes!" Melissa said, "I was stunned. I was mad. I was embarrassed."

"What do you mean I talked too much?" she asked him. He said: "You spent so much time selling her on the idea of the gift that you missed her commitment [to make the gift]."

Her supervisor's feedback shook her like an earthquake. "Is this how I have approached every other donor meeting that I've ever had?" She reflected: "I've been talking too much. How many gifts have I missed over the course of time because I simply talked through it?"

Overall, Melissa took her boss's feedback well. "I was fortunate that I worked with someone who was honest with me," she said, "and he shared some tips and some tricks. But "it dawned on me that I was not listening," she said with disappointment. "I was simply listening to respond and I was not listening to understand." From that moment on, Melissa vowed to listen more deeply.

This chapter is about learning to make the shift that Melissa made in her own life. As described in the "Wheel of Positive Communication," our final principle is **when you choose to listen deeply, you can transcend the perceived differences that exist between you and others.** Listening deeply, we argue in this chapter, is at the heart of effective leadership. We will show you how to do it well and how to apply it to your role as a leader. First, you will learn the key elements of deep listening and how to put those into action immediately. Then, you will develop the skills to navigate common barriers to deep listening. Finally, we show you how to leverage those skills to create a culture of deep listening across your organization.

LEVEL I: THE POWER OF LISTENING DEEPLY

Listening matters in our personal relationships, but it's also a highly desirable workplace skill. When leaders listen deeply to their stakeholders, they naturally promote open communication and benefit from "stronger perceptions of supportiveness, motivation, increased employee productivity, and lower absenteeism."[1] As professionals move up the chain of command, listening well becomes even more crucial. One study found that top executives "spend approximately twice as much time listening as other employees" and that as "workers make the transition into upper-level management, they rely more on listening to perform effectively."[2] In short, the higher you want to go, the more important listening will become.

The higher leaders go in an organization,
the more time they spend listening.

Michael Schwartz's story shows what can happen when we commit to listening. Michael is dean of the McGeorge School of Law. Under his leadership, the school has seen amazing successes, including a recent $25 million gift from a major donor. Enrollment at his school has been skyrocketing, the budget is balanced, the bar pass rate is the highest in 25 years, and the job placement rate is the highest in the history of the school. In other words, he and his team are doing a pretty good job. In addition to being effective, Michael exemplifies positive leadership. For example, every year, he sends a personal note to every new law school student who has been admitted. He says, "I read their personal statements and I respond to something specific." He also makes sure to send a special thank you to every single faculty and staff member at the law school. He loves to walk around the campus and meet people face to face. In our recent conversation with Michael, he revealed his approach to listening.

In our interview, we asked him: "So, how do you create an environment where people feel heard?" He said: "If you ask me *what is the bottom line?* I have to be honest with you. It's simply shutting up." Michael offered an example. "[A while back] I was just meeting with the law school unity's caucus. I'm not sure I did a great job listening [then] because I was anxious and my anxiety was causing me to talk too much," he reflected. In a more recent meeting, "I started by saying: 'Look, I'm here to give you the space to make this meeting be whatever you want it to be.' And then I stopped talking."

"The interesting thing is," he said, "I'm not sure that I ended up speaking less because they would ask me questions, but the experience was different. Essentially, they were in control of the direction of the meeting and me not trying to control it." He crystallizes the moment: "I surrendered to the flow." With this story in mind, use box 7.1 to reflect about your own experience with deep listening.

Letting go of control and surrendering to the moment is an inherent part of learning to listen more deeply. Years ago, Julien conducted an interview for his book *How Communication Scholars Think and Act* with Arvind Singhal. We mentioned Arvind in a previous chapter. He is a professor of communication at the University of Texas at El Paso. Arvind has traveled the globe to help small and large communities create change. In an interview with Julien, he shared that he used to have only two ways of responding when the conversation got tough. His first response was the fight response. If the meeting was becoming difficult or he felt that it was not going in the right direction,

Box 7.1. **What Do the Best Listeners Do?**

Instructions: Reflect for a moment about a time when someone in your life truly listened to you. How did the interaction unfold? What did the other person *do* to make you feel heard? Check the elements of great listening that apply to your situation:

- ☐ The other person was fully present with me and completely in the moment.
- ☐ The other person was open to my thoughts, ideas, and feelings.
- ☐ The other person showed that they understood my experience from my vantage point.
- ☐ The other person was genuine and showed that they cared.

Draw on this experience to approach your most difficult moments. When it comes to listening well, what you *actually* do matters more than what you've heard about listening.

he would fight for his way. He would argue and would try to win. Sometimes he used a second response: the flight response. He would withdraw from the interaction and become more and more disengaged. But with experience, he developed a third way: to lean into the moment and become curious about the interaction. This is what he said in the interview: "I make that effort today to listen . . . truly listen and to shut up about what's going on. . . . I'm telling myself 'Just shut up, just let it happen,' embrace the lessons, lean into the discomfort. Don't fight it. Lean into it if you can. Be vulnerable for a moment because then you are fully present."[3]

Listening more deeply is a leadership skill. The crux of the problem is how to develop that skill. In this section, you'll learn three interrelated elements of deep listening you can practice in your own communication right away.

Habit 1: Be Fully Present

As you can see from Michael's and Arvind's stories, deep listening requires each of us to be fully present. Being fully present means being physically engaged by leaning in and squaring the shoulder toward the other person. It means giving others our full attention with our bodies, our minds, and our focus.

There is a nice short story we like from Mitch Albom in his book *Have a Little Faith* that illustrates this point. The story goes like this. A little girl comes home and is excited to share her drawing with her mother. She comes into the kitchen where her mom is preparing dinner and tending to the pots and says, "Look Mom! I've drawn something beautiful." She is so excited to share what she's done. In response, her mom takes a quick glance, nods her head, and returns to the pots, saying, "It looks great honey." The little girl, however, is not impressed and says, "Mom, I'm really proud of this drawing. Take a look." And the mom does the same thing. She takes a quick look, says, "It looks really good honey," and returns to her cooking. This upsets the girl. She says, "Mom, you're not listening to me!" The mom says, "I am listening to you, baby." "No," the little girl says, "you're not listening to me with your eyes."[4] Deep listening demonstrates an "all in" approach that gives the other person your full attention.

In her article on deep listening and leadership, Laura Brearly wrote: "When we are present, we are available to tune into other people and to our context."[5] In his work, Otto Scharmer described the experience of deep listening with the concept of "presencing," which means both being present and sensing one's environment. It means "opening a space in which genuine contact can be made."[6] The concept of deep listening cuts across time, cultures, and contexts. In the African tradition, for instance, Brearly explained that the Swahili word *Sikia* translates as "integrated sensing, in which "one simultaneously sees and hears, pays attention to, notices, understands, and perceives."[7] In Chinese Buddhist tradition, the characters that compose the phrase "deep listening" involve the concepts "listen" and "respect" and include the "ideas of Heaven, People, Earth, Ear, Eye, Heart" and other rich imagery.[8] Clearly, deep listening sets high expectations!

One of the biggest gifts you can offer your people is to be fully present. Create a space where you and the other person will not be disrupted. Put away your phone or move away from the computer so that you can give the other person your full attention. It can also be helpful to have a notepad and pen ready and to take some notes about what the other person says. Collectively, these small behaviors show the other person that you are committed to listening and what they are saying is important to you.

One of the biggest gifts you can offer your people is to be fully present.

We recently interviewed Jerry, vice president and director of transportation for an engineering company. Jerry is responsible for hundreds of employees and well-respected in his field. He is well-known as a kind and respectful leader who seeks to grow and develop his employees. He also loves to be part of a winning team. Jerry talked about listening as a key component of great leadership. He said, "I have to work on listening." One effective strategy he uses is taking notes. He said, "I take a lot of notes during my meetings and as I hear thoughts, I'm writing stuff down. . . . I put red dots around critical information and tell myself, 'Okay, we need to come back to that.'"

Jerry often follows up to clarify critical information. He role-played how he'd say it in a normal conversation. "'Hey Julien,'" he demonstrated, "'you mentioned this earlier and I'm not sure I understand that fully.' Or 'Help me understand what you meant by that.' I'll do that a lot to [help me] listen better." Jerry approaches the conversations with a dose of humility and humor. He'll sometimes say, "I know you said this already, and everybody else on the call understood perfectly, but I'm slow. I'm like a six-year-old." Then he will add, "But it's really important that I understand this because you need my support to move forward. And once I understand it fully, you're not going to have a bigger advocate than me."

Jerry shows, in other words, that he is present and committed to listening completely. He is fully engaged in the conversation. That's deep listening. It means really being with the other person, pushing away all distractions, and listening with your eyes and with your pen.

Habit 2: Open Your Mind, Heart, and Hand

Listening deeply means experiencing a higher degree of openness. When Julien explains the nature of deep listening in presentations, he asks the audience to join him in this quick exercise: "Take your right hand and make a really tight fist. Imagine that this is the frustration you are feeling in a meeting that is not going well or a one-on-one visit with an employee that has gone wrong. Now take your right hand and very slowly open it so that the palm of your hand is facing up." "This," Julien will say, "is the whole story of listening. Listening is all about accepting ideas; it's all about opening your hand."

Openness is about welcoming new ideas, new perspectives, and new ways of thinking. Remaining open does not mean you abandon your point of view. Openness is about maintaining a fine balance between holding our own perspective and "being profoundly open to others."[9] Cultivating one's ability to be open to new ideas and experiences has a range of positive benefits and outcomes. Openness is connected to intelligence, creativity, and a person's ability to be influential. People with a high degree of openness are also often viewed in positive ways and experience higher satisfaction in relationships.

At the same time, openness is difficult for some people to develop. Openness involves our ability to accept and welcome new information. As one of our interviewees for this book said, "Leaders, in general, are very stubborn. They believe in something and they keep on pushing whether people agree or disagree." He added: "But I have found that listening deeply has given me a new perspective." Gaining fresh perspective, even if one may not fully change their view, is obviously critical for leaders. They must be open to hearing new ideas, thoughts, and constructs so they can innovate, adapt, and thrive.

Habit 3: Show Empathy

Listening connects us to others and builds relationships. As Henry Cloud showed, "When we are emotionally and relationally connected to others, stress levels in the brain diminish. Put simply, relationships change brain chemistry."[10] One hallmark of effective relationship development is listening with empathy, a leader's ability to imagine and understand others' experiences. In the realm of listening, Carl Rogers, the renowned psychologist, used the phrase "empathetic understanding" to describe our willingness and ability to understand another person's thoughts, feelings, and struggles.[11]

Recent research has shown that there is an effective model leaders can use to listen with empathy. It is called active-empathic listening (AEL) and builds upon the work of Carl Rogers.[12] Research has shown that employees who work with leaders who practice AEL "are more satisfied with their work and report higher overall well-being."[13] To listen more deeply, the AEL strategy has three main steps. You'll notice that many of the listening examples in the chapter so far illustrate these behaviors.

The first step is **sensing**. This means to be completely attentive and involved in the moment. Sensing is being fully present with your heart, your mind, and your body. It is positioning yourself to show the other that you are sensitive to what they are saying. You show you understand how others feel. You listen to both what is being said and what is left unsaid. It's also about creating a sense of focus. You can accomplish this by

✓ moving away from your desk and sitting with a person around a coffee table;

✓ putting away your phone;

✓ asking your administrative assistant, if you have one, to hold all calls or other interruptions; and

✓ giving the other person your undivided attention.

The second step is **processing**. This is any attempt on your part to reassure the other person that you are in fact listening deeply. You may share direct assurances that you will remember what they say. This can be accomplished in the following ways:

✓ Provide direct reassurances such as "I want to make sure that I understand you fully."

✓ Write down notes to show the other person that you are present and working to remember their message.

✓ Check for meaning: "Tell me more about what you mean when you said . . . ."

✓ Acknowledge and speak out loud the points of agreement and the points of disagreement between you and the other person: "I see three areas where we seem to agree and one area in which we have a disagreement. What do you think?"

All of these behaviors are designed to show the other person that you are indeed listening deeply.

The third step is **responding**. Here, you use your communication skills to acknowledge other people's ideas. Responding involves behaviors such as nodding or leaning in. More importantly, it includes actions that demonstrate understanding. You can achieve this step by doing the following:

✓ Ask direct questions to probe and check for understanding: "Tell me more about what this means from your perspective."

✓ Restate what the other person has said. For instance, "If I heard you correctly, you are having a very difficult time at work. You feel lost about your role, and you need clearer expectations. I can understand how this would be difficult for you. I think I can help now."

Listening with empathy will change your leadership style. In a recent interview, Amare shared a story about a powerful moment between her and a family member. Her story demonstrates the way empathy can transform family relationships as well.[14]

"I had a breakthrough with a family member recently," Amare said. "For years, I had really tried to let the past be the past. I thought I had forgiven this person, but I realized that I probably really had not." She took a moment to collect her thoughts.

"I was still angry and I was still bitter. I couldn't let go. I couldn't say 'Okay, I totally forgive you.' I was not able to listen to what they were saying because I was always on the other end thinking, 'Well, this is what you did to me,'" she said with force. "I couldn't accept what she was trying to tell me."

Then, Amare made an intentional shift.

"I was able to give this person a chance. I was able to become open."

She changed her mindset as a listener. She tried to see, hear, and feel the experience. Amare said, "Okay, I'm going to let you tell me. I'm going to take my opinions and my preconceived ideas about what I think you think, and I'm really just going to listen to you."

"And then, I was able to share with her," she explained. "I didn't really want to share [in the past] with this person because I felt like sharing with her would give her ammunition to hurt me. I decided to just let that go and try it. It was really the first time I actually listened to her and I let her tell me what she felt." That shift planted the seeds of empathy and opened the door for mutual understanding.

As she listened, so did her family member.

"I shared [too]," she said. "And I was completely honest, but not in a way to hurt her, but saying this is truly how I feel."

And then the magic happened. Her family member reacted, "Oh, I get it." "It was the first time she ever really heard me [and] it was the first time I was really able to hear her. From that time forward," Amare explained, "our relationship has really changed and evolved and I don't feel that anger and bitterness anymore. It's gone. It feels so good not to be carrying that around, not to have that on my shoulders anymore."

When people listen to one another more deeply, they become more connected. They transcend their perceived differences. "Real communication," Carl Rogers explained, "occurs when we listen with understanding. When we listen deeply."[15] But getting there is difficult. Having laid the foundation of what deep listening is, we focus next on how you can draw on the power of deep listening to handle the most difficult moments. We highlight the common barriers that prohibit each of us from engaging more meaningfully and show you how you can overcome them to establish common ground at the individual and the group levels.

LEVEL 2: TRANSCEND DIFFERENCES

Listening well is one of the key ways to transcend the differences between individuals. And yet whenever we talk about listening in workshops or classes, inevitably somebody will say some version of the following: "This makes sense. I want to listen deeply and completely. I want to be fully present and empathize. The problem is, I get distracted. I get riled up by what people say. I have so many other thoughts." Clearly there's a very practical side to a skill like listening. To do it well, we must learn to overcome common listening barriers so we can then transcend the differences we feel between ourselves and others. We share four leadership barriers to listening and then discuss how to overcome them.

Barrier 1: Jumping to Conclusions

If you jump to conclusions, you're not alone. As Rogers explained, "The major barrier to mutual interpersonal communication is our very natural tendency to judge, to evaluate, to approve or disapprove, the statement of the other person, or the other group."[16] Many of us seem to naturally judge what we hear almost instantly without hearing the entire message. This is especially true for leaders because we spend most of our days diagnosing and solving the various problems people bring us. The trouble with reaching conclusions too soon in a conversation is that it short-circuits our ability to listen well and can make people feel dismissed. It's very difficult, for instance, to make up your mind and empathize at the same time.

Alex once coached an executive who consistently fast-forwarded to the end of conversations in team meetings. Reaching the final conclusion of the matter was all she seemed to care about. She'd listen to a follower for just a few moments, anticipate where the conversation was headed, and interrupt with a possible solution. To her credit, she was correct about the problem and solution more often than not. The trouble was, even when she was right, her followers still needed more time to think aloud and catch up with her. A director above her explained, "She needs to slow down and allow her team the time they need to process the situation. Even if her team members end up in the exact same spot that she would have recommended in the first place, they will have benefited from going through it, thinking aloud, and learning from the discussion rather than skipping to the end." Thankfully, the executive learned to hold her peace and listen more fully before reaching conclusions. She was then able to be patient and present for her followers in a more complete way. Her team members also appreciated her new tendency to listen more completely.

√ **To avoid jumping to conclusions, slow down the process of communication.**

Barrier 2: Making Assumptions about the Other Person

The assumptions we make about others form an instant barrier. Assumptions act like a filter that can make us miss important details or even the heart of the message. We may notice the way a person dresses, talks, or carries themselves, and we mentally fill in the rest of the blanks about them and the opinions they likely hold. We might "size them up," put people in a mental category, and unfairly make up our minds about them. It's almost impossible to transcend our differences when we are preoccupied by them. In a previous job, Alex once supervised Nelson. He had lots of piercings, multicolored hair done in a style that resembled a mohawk, torn-up clothing, and numerous visible tattoos. Although these defining characteristics are more widely accepted today, at the time there was no doubt that Nelson stood out from others on the team. It was easy to glance quickly at those specific surface-level features and make assumptions about his qualities or characteristics. Most of those assumptions would have been dead wrong. This is usually the case when we assume that individuals conform to group stereotypes. Making assumptions would have made Alex miss what Nelson had to offer.

It's almost impossible to transcend our differences when we are preoccupied by them.

By the end of just a couple of conversations, Alex could see that Nelson was empathetic and cared a lot about other people. He was an excellent listener, lighthearted, genuinely humorous, and charismatic. He also had a high-paying job as an in-demand software developer and showed clear entrepreneurial tendencies. Instead of allowing our assumptions about others to take root, it's better to leave generous amounts of space in our minds and see that each person is a unique individual. Only then can we see all they have to offer. Listening with that open mindset rather than making assumptions will allow us to be fully present.

√ **To avoid making assumptions about the other,
discover similarities and expand your degree of empathy.**

Barrier 3: Listening in Order to Reply

A third barrier is the habit of listening in order to reply rather than listening to understand. This was the exact barrier Melissa was experiencing in the story that opened this chapter. Well-known author Stephen Covey talked about the tendency of many people to mentally prepare their rebuttals or responses rather than investing their energy in understanding what the other person is saying.[17] It's virtually impossible to listen well and rehearse your own point at the same time. At a minimum, this will lead to misunderstandings or even mischaracterizations of the other person's point. Listening in order to reply can also make interactions feel more like an unnecessary debate or a conflict rather than a helpful conversation. Thankfully, there is a way to battle this tendency.

In one interview, we spent some time with Mahendra, a senior vice president for a global nonprofit organization. In our conversation, he emphasized the importance of listening. He described how a leader could engage in what he called reflective listening to prevent his tendency to listen in order to respond. He said, "Listening is more than physical listening. It's more of a reflection. It's just trying to look from where this person is coming from using their lens." "Your goal," he explained, "is to understand and acknowledge and reach out." Instead of focusing on his response, he commits his focus to fully understanding first. For example, he said he might say to the person: "You know what, the other day you said that and it didn't get through to me, but I kept on thinking, and this is my learning, this is what came from my reflection. Does that resonate with what you're thinking? Am I a little bit off track?" "Now," he said, "the person is overwhelmingly engaged in the conversation. And since I have also put some reflection and thinking [into the conversation], I'm also finding it meaningful to chat on that topic."

That's what it looks like to listen with reflection instead of responding automatically. Mahendra said listening this way "has given me a new perspective, even if I may not deviate from the overall goal or my own vision of what is true and what's not true. A lot of times people don't agree with me and that's fine. I respect their experience, but listening requires reflection."

A friend and colleague, Allan Ward, used a similar approach to make sure he understood before he responded. Allan served for years as a professor and colleague but was best known for his activities during the civil rights movement, when he led hard conversations with families and groups to confront racism and prejudice. You can read about some of Allan's experiences in the book *Civil Rights Brothers*. He once taught us, "We don't respond to the reality around us through our senses as we do to our concept of that reality." This is why he developed a clear strategy to check for mutual understanding and meaning, a practice that echoes what Mahendra practiced as a leader. Allan once explained, "I found myself increasingly even in private conversations asking, 'What do you mean by that word?' 'Well, here's the way I was brought up with that word,' someone might reply." Then, he would say, "Given what we are talking about, what would be the best definition for us when we are talking about this?" Allan discovered that probing patiently and becoming curious about the meaning of words or phrases people used was one of his go-to listening habits. He said, "I found that checking for meaning became very comfortable, almost a necessity, so we are talking about the same thing."[18] Good listeners put aside their desire to reply instantly. Instead, they simply commit to understanding the other person.

√ **To avoid the trap of replying too quickly,
ask a few key questions first.**

Barrier 4: Drifting

Mental "drift" is the last listening barrier. Imagine that you're having a conversation and the other person mentions a word in passing. The word might have little to do with the main point of the conversation. It could be any word that reminds you of something else. Your mind then drifts off in that other direction for a moment or two. By the time you realize that you've drifted off and snap out of it, you have already missed at least part of what the other person said. You're a step behind, and you know it. Sound familiar?

Almost any word can make our minds wander. Still, we tend to drift off more when we hear words or topics that matter to us. In worst-case-scenarios, something we hear pushes a button and our emotions escalate. We ALL have hot-button words or topics, for better or for worse. Political topics, sports teams, and office gossip are common examples. If we let our tendency to drift off get the best of us like this, our listening skills will suffer noticeably. The key is to have the discipline to notice your tendency to drift as soon as it happens rather than indulging it. Make a habit out of snapping yourself out of the drift. Remind yourself about the speaker's main point. And return to using good active listening skills to keep yourself on track, like asking a relevant question or reflecting back what you hear the other person saying to keep yourself engaged. By actively participating, your mind will refocus and prevent further drift.

> √ **To avoid mental drifting, reflect back what**
> **you heard and physically lean in.**

Take stock of the challenges you have faced when listening to others by reviewing box 7.2. If you can manage these listening barriers and make even modest improvements in overcoming them, you will be better positioned to transcend the differences and perceived distance between ourselves and others. You are ready to find common ground.

Finding Common Ground

Managing our own listening barriers is an essential listening skill, but it's only a prerequisite. One of the main goals of listening deeply is to look for and create common ground in conversations. Common ground is the foundation of friendships, collaboration, and teamwork. It allows us to work together with excellence.

Box 7.2. **Which Deep Listening Barriers Do You Experience?**

Instructions: Check the box next to any of the listening barriers you experience that prevent deep listening.

☐ Jumping to conclusions
☐ Making assumptions about the other person
☐ Preparing a reply rather than focusing on the other's person message
☐ Drifting

Given the box(es) you checked off, which listening barrier do you need to improve on most? Look again at the strategies we offered and write down what you will focus on here:

Here is where we see the critical role of communication come into even clearer focus. At its root, the Latin word *communicare* means, in part, "to make common," "to share," "to unite." From a practical standpoint, the process of communicating with others is to create shared meaning, a shared understanding, and metaphorical common ground. That's one of the reasons that most discussions about listening emphasize empathy, because its aim is to understand and feel what the other person is feeling. When we listen well, in other words, we should be on the lookout for common interests, values, and priorities. Too often we get stuck talking about surface-level opinions that can derail a conversation and turn it into an unnecessary debate or conflict.

That's why Roger Fisher and William Ury explained the difference between *positions* and *interests* in their classic book *Getting to Yes*.[19] For example, as a supervisor, you might take the specific position in a conversation that you want one of your most influential team members to come to work in person rather than working from home so often. In response, this team member may dig in their heels and insist that they must work from home. If you both stay focused on those two fixed positions, you have no common ground to work with, and you're not likely to find a solution. However, if you listen for the interest beneath the team member's desire to work from home, you may find some common ground. Listening deeply, for example, might reveal that the primary interest that is driving the team member's I-must-work-from-home position is their desire to be with their aging dog, who currently needs more attention. By listening carefully to the interests *beneath* their position, you can almost instantly discover common ground and a pathway forward that everybody could be happy with. A quick revision to the team's pet policy, for instance, could allow team members the freedom to bring dogs to work. This could very well satisfy everybody's interests in this scenario. When we listen for common ground, we'll notice themes like desire for respect, appreciation, growth, opportunity, advancement, and many other needs most people want out of life. Discovering these deeper needs requires patient listening, a patience that is particularly important during difficult conversations, when you can feel the emotional temperature in the room rising.

**√ To find common ground, listen closely to
the other person's interests *beneath* their position**

Another powerful way to transcend difference is to appreciate the deeper shared experience we all have as human beings. As the old expression goes, "We all want the same things." In short, we all want some version of happy, healthy, and meaningful lives. As leaders, it's important to remind ourselves of those common experiences so we don't miss the humanity we see in others. Years ago, author and philosopher Martin Buber made some important points about how we can transcend our differences. At the heart of many communication problems is our tendency to view other people narrowly. We often see ourselves as well-rounded, whole human beings, but in contrast, we tend to see others as comparatively one-dimensional. We don't deliberately desire to simplify how we characterize others. We do it almost by default. We get busy. We have our own pressures and problems to deal with. In a nutshell, we get self-centered. We then use mental shortcuts to generalize or even stereotype others to deal with them more efficiently. This is not an ideal leadership behavior, but it's important to first recognize our own unhelpful tendencies to view other people in one dimension. Next, we have to remind ourselves that we are talking with whole human beings who are, in many ways, a lot like us. They have inherent value and deserve our attention and respect.[20]

Pausing for a few seconds helps us see others as whole human beings who are also struggling. This instantly softens our touch.

We also all face similar obstacles to pursuing the things we want. Consider a typical trip to the grocery store. You are already tired from working all day. You have a long list of items to find. The store is crowded and difficult to navigate. The entire shopping process takes too long and costs too much. The line at the register is five shoppers deep, and their shopping carts are all overflowing. By the time you reach the cashier, it's very difficult to view that employee as a whole human being. You would not be the only one who sees them as a cashier who has one job, to get you out of the store as efficiently as possible. It would be totally understandable if most shoppers in this situation did not take the time to slow down their thought process, put themselves in the shoes of the cashier, and imagine what their day has been like. And yet, pausing for a few seconds helps us see others as whole human beings who are also struggling. This instantly softens our touch. If we did that, we'd see that the cashier has also had a stressful shift and a long list of life pressures on their mind. If we recognized the common humanity, experiences, and obstacles we share, we'd feel our empathy for the cashier increase and our attitude ease.

The really important kind of freedom involves attention, awareness, and discipline, as well as being able truly to care about other people and to sacrifice for them over and over in myriad petty, unsexy ways every day.

—David Foster Wallace

Seeing others as whole human beings may sound like a tall order, but we've all seen at least some individuals around us connect empathetically with others like this even during stressful and time-pressured situations. Granted, it's not reasonable to expect that we would pause and connect like this in every conversation all day with every cashier, bus driver, bank teller, or crossing guard. Many interactions are not meant to last more than a few seconds, and that's expected. Still, a tendency to see others as well-rounded human beings with inherent dignity is a powerful way to live life, lead at work, and transcend our differences.

√ **To find common ground, identify the similarities
between your experience and the other's experience.**

As a leader, you can avoid the common barriers that all of us face in our
attempts to listen more deeply and find the common ground. Next, we build
on this set of skills to level up your leadership and establish a listening culture
across the organization. Before continuing to the next level, review box 7.3 to
reflect about moments in which you have been a successful listener.

Box 7.3. **Your Success as a Listener**

Instructions: Take a moment now to reflect on the elements of deep
listening. Take some time to respond to the following prompt and write
down how you successfully listened more deeply.

Please write a story about a time when you had a difficult conversation with someone and you were proud of what you accomplished in
the conversation. What is the story, and what made the breakthrough
or success possible?

Notes:

LEVEL 3: ESTABLISH A LISTENING CULTURE

You now have the foundation to listen more deeply. As President Woodrow
Wilson once said, "The ear of the leader must ring with the voices of the
people." These interpersonal skills will help you as a leader stay open, show
empathy and understanding, and create a place where each person can feel

heard and valued. You have the tools to overcome common listening obstacles that hinder all of us and some ways to create common ground.

It's time now to level up those skills across your team. Researchers Jay Flynn, Tuula-Riitta Valikoski, and Jenni Grau published an overview of decades' worth of research on listening in the business sector.[21] They explained the importance of team-wide listening: "Effective workplace listening is not simply limited to the skills that employees do or do not possess. It also includes the idea of organizational listening, the environment in which listening occurs that is shaped by the organization." It's up to the leader to create a culture of listening. Doing so creates real benefits. These authors showed that listening across the organization will "boost employee morale, increase cooperation, improve productivity, educate employees, and reduce employee turnover and potential lawsuits."[22] In this section, we feature three team-wide approaches you can use to create this listening culture. It's up to you to bring it to life. Use box 7.4 to check what you have already done as a leader before moving on to the next section.

Box 7.4. How Do You Listen Widely to Your Stakeholders?

Instructions: Take a moment to reflect on what you have already done to create a deep listening culture across your organization. Put a check mark next to any communication habits you can confidently say you have accomplished in your role as a leader.

- ☐ I create an intentional space on meeting agendas to listen to my stakeholders.
- ☐ I meet frequently with people to gather their input and their ideas.
- ☐ I use various strategies to make sure I hear from less vocal team members.
- ☐ I have recently conducted a listening tour with all of my stakeholders.
- ☐ I have recently polled my employees with a survey and discussed the findings with relevant stakeholders.

Using your responses, focus your reading in the next section on areas that you can improve on.

Strategy 1: Put Listening Space on Meeting Agendas

One effective way to weave listening into your leadership approach and your team's culture is to put it on the meeting agenda. If you are leading your team, then you directly shape the way meetings are run. We recommend that you literally make listening part of your prepared agenda for important one-on-one and group meetings. In most cases, leaders do a fair job of preparing the information they need to distribute and talk about with their teams. It's less common to see a leader reserve adequate time to listen carefully and process the opinions and concerns followers express. In fact, we've seen many leaders treat legitimate questions and concerns as obstacles to so-called progress. To fix this, simply adding a bullet point like "Listen to opinions" or "Listening Moment" to important agenda items would remind both leaders and followers that listening is an important part of the way the team works.

Some leaders we know make it a point to dedicate entire specific periodic one-on-one meetings to listening. In fact, a very successful executive coach Julien and Alex know shared that she intentionally creates space for high-level executives to think aloud in a private, low-risk context. In most cases, she said, "They already know the answers or at least have it in them some potential ways to move forward. They just need me to be there, reflect what I'm hearing, and ask some thoughtful questions. . . . I find that I end up listening about 80% of the time." As leaders, we can use this same coaching approach for at least some of our group and one-on-one meetings by putting listening on the written agenda.

Strategy 2: Use the 1-2-4-All Method

Most team discussions follow a typical pattern: the most vocal people speak up and think on their feet, the less vocal people form their thoughts more patiently. As a result, the less vocal people often miss their opportunity because by the time they have chosen the right words, the conversation has already moved on to something else. By the end of most group discussions, the prevailing viewpoint usually reflects just a fraction of team members' interests. In other words, many groups don't slow down and take the time to build real listening from all parties into their process. You can break this pattern by using the 1-2-4-All method.

The 1-2-4-All method is a simple and effective approach developed by Henri Lipmanowicz and Keith McCandless to slow down communication and spark conversations that would not naturally occur.[23] (You can learn more about these techniques by visiting liberatingstructures.com).

Here's how 1-2-4-All works. Imagine you are leading a retreat with your leadership team to develop a set of values for the organization, tweak your mission statement, and strengthen your vision. Here is what you do to engage everyone and build on their contributions.

The first part of this process, "1," provides time for individual reflection. Set aside time for each person on the leadership team to reflect on and answer whatever specific written questions you have. For instance, you might dedicate 15 to 20 minutes or more to letting everybody in the room answer these questions on their own:

1. What core values do you think should ground our work as a leadership team? Please write down five.
2. From your perspective, what should be the revised mission statement? Please write a draft of the mission statement as you would like it.
3. From your vantage point, what are three dream goals that we should execute in the next five years?

It's critical that you give people enough time on their own to draft their answers. Do not skip this important step, because it provides the less vocal individuals time to prepare their thoughts.

The second step is "2." Here, the leader puts people in pairs and asks them to share with one another what they wrote and to work collaboratively. The goal of talking in pairs is to create a more personal space for people to express themselves. This ensures that everyone has the opportunity to contribute. In this step, however, members of the pairs need to collaboratively arrive at a mutually satisfying proposal. In a discussion on values, mission, and vision, you would frame the questions this way:

1. As a pair, what are the four top values that you both agree should guide our work?
2. As a pair, what would be your proposed mission statement?
3. As a pair, what are three goals that we should execute in the next five years?

Notice how the questions are designed to nudge the pairs to deliberate and make choices. Together, they bring ten values to the table. They must eliminate at least six of their combined choices to identify the top four. This process allows for true collaboration.

Next is "4." After talking in pairs, form groups of four. The discussion in groups of four is the same as it was in pairs. You ask the group to talk through the values, mission, and vision. For example, you might ask each group to take their separate lists and work together to choose the top five values they believe are the most important. Similarly, you would ask the group to work through the mission and vision statements. The process is gradually moving from *intrapersonal* communication (i.e., conversation with oneself), to *interpersonal* communication (i.e., conversation with another person), to *group* communication. The process involves numerous rounds of careful listening.

The last step is "All." At this phase, the conversation now includes everyone. The subgroups of four now all pitch their drafts to the entire team in search of commonalities and differences. Together, the team works toward common ground that ultimately leads the group to agree on a focused set of values, a mission statement, and a set of goals for the next five years.

What makes 1-2-4-All so effective is that it includes everyone in the process and gives each person numerous opportunities to engage and be heard. Through conversations and dialogue like this, groups often realize that they are more similar than different. It is a process that cultivates deep listening.

Strategy 3: Collect Data and Experiences from Your Stakeholders

Scholars and practitioners have long agreed that the art of listening is inseparable from good leadership. As researcher Andrew Wolvin explained, "A listening leader communicates with his/her followers in order to understand their needs, motivations, and issues. These understandings serve as the foundation for solid decision-making to further the relationship/organization to its goals."[24] Listening is not a flashy skill when we think about how it compares to giving a keynote presentation. Still, many high-level leaders emphasize the importance of listening. Joseph Neubauer, ARAMARK's former CEO, once said, "By listening to [employees] and earning their commitment, we identified opportunities, reshaped our culture to embrace innovation and pursue growth, and got back on track."[25] Lee Iacocca, former CEO of Chrysler Corporation, said, "You have to be able to listen well if you're going to motivate the people who work for you. Right there, that's the difference between a mediocre company and a great company."[26]

One major struggle leaders at all levels face is that they end up listening mainly to the people right around them or to individuals who feel most comfortable speaking up. In a research class, we might say that this results in "skewed data" or a "biased sample." For example, Alex was approached several times in a forty-eight-hour period by a faculty member who was complaining about some wording in a document his department was revising. The teacher claimed urgently, "Everybody is really bothered by this. We really need to change this wording right away." Alex listened patiently and did his best to understand the nuances of the faculty member's point, but something seemed off. He had already met with numerous other faculty members that week and had open conversations, and nobody else had mentioned the issue. He thought to himself, "Everybody is complaining? That doesn't sound right." Rather than make the requested change without the team's input, he raised the question openly at the next departmental meeting to listen to everybody's actual opinion rather than secondhand reports. As it turned out, the faculty member who initially complained about the document's wording was the only one who thought it was a problem. Nobody else wanted to change the wording. It's not clear whether this was a deliberate attempt by the faculty member to manipulate the situation or a simple misunderstanding. Either way, the discussion put the issue to rest, and the faculty member politely dropped the request. Had Alex simply trusted the opinion of this one individual, he would have made a decision that was out of touch with what the overwhelming majority of team members wanted. It's not a good idea to give the chronic complainers' voices more weight than they deserve. We advocate here for two simple ways to listen to a healthy cross-section or representative sample of followers.

First, schedule a listening tour. By definition, a listening tour is "a set period of time where the new manager meets with as many key stakeholders as possible to ask questions, hear concerns, identify barriers, and build rapport."[27] Despite the size of your responsibilities, department, and unit, you need to create opportunities to meet with as many stakeholders as possible as soon as you are in a role.

The primary goal of a listening tour is to listen deeply to your internal and external stakeholders. In a 2017 *New York Times* article, Adam Bryant interviewed the CEO of Levi Strauss and Company.[28] In the interview, Chip

Bergh shared how he ran his own listening tour when he took over the company. He recalled the following:

> When I first got here, I interviewed the top 60 people in the company, and I sent them questions in advance, including:
>
> - What are the three things you think we have to change?
> - What are the three things that we have to keep?
> - What do you most want me to do?
> - What are you most afraid I might do?

Bergh continued, "I had an hour scheduled for each of them, and by the end, I was really clear about the company's DNA, and the values that were really important to everyone who works here."

For his listening tour, he also selected a particular segment of his stakeholders and guided one-on-one conversations with a clear focus. If you do a listening tour, create a plan that includes a cross-section and the right mixture of followers so you are confident about the quality of information you will hear.

Second, gauge attitudes and beliefs from your stakeholders with surveys. When surveys are done well, the data provides leaders with a high-quality and balanced snapshot of issues followers believe are going well or not so well. There's an endless list of potential issues you could ask your followers about, including general satisfaction surveys or issue-specific surveys like the employee engagement surveys or the organization's crisis and renewal preparedness surveys mentioned in earlier chapters. Some leaders are courageous enough to give followers surveys with direct questions about their leadership approach (e.g., "How satisfied are you with my leadership approach?" "How could I improve as a leader?").

The real purpose of conducting surveys is to listen more deeply to your stakeholders about important items. Surveys don't look like traditional listening, but they can be just as helpful. As scholars have explained, "Conducting employee surveys does not, on its own, constitute listening. But hearing and fully receiving the thoughts, feelings, ideas, concerns, and emotions of others from them directly does."[29] Leaders can carefully consider survey results and use them to make informed decisions, create change, and meet the needs of followers.

Now it's time to implement these changes in your everyday practice.

LEVEL 4: PUT IT INTO PRACTICE

Let's narrow this chapter down to some practical, actionable steps you can take. Following are some reminders of ways you can make listening a top priority to make your workplace a more positive environment. Circle the top takeaways that you could most easily put into practice.

Listen Deeply

- **Be fully present.** Devote your full attention and focus when listening to others. This can start with your mindset but should also be demonstrated in your nonverbal communication. Lean in and orient your shoulders toward the person. Make eye contact and listen completely.
- **Open your mind, heart, and hand.** A great way to stay open while listening is to do the brief unclenched fist exercise. During difficult conversations, discreetly clench your fist. Gradually relax your hand until it is fully open in a palm-up position. Use this exercise to put yourself in a more open state of mind and then stay there.
- **Show empathy.** Listen to understand the other person on their own terms. Put yourself in their shoes so you can understand where they are coming from. Use active listening skills to help you stay focused and to show the other person that you are paying attention and making a sincere effort to enter their world.

Transcend Difference

- **Identify common listening barriers.** Listening sounds easy enough in theory. In practice, we are often thrown off our game by common barriers like jumping to conclusions, making assumptions about the speaker, listening in order to reply, and letting our minds drift off when we hear words that push our hot buttons. Instead of indulging your bad listening habits, take time to identify your tendencies and use the tips in this chapter to give others your best.
- **Find common ground.** Look for common ground when listening. Common ground is a prerequisite for working excellently together. Look past surface-level positions and listen for the deeper interests and common experiences you share with others as human beings. At the root of

communication is the shared meaning and shared understanding you can create with others.

Establish a Listening Culture

- **Put listening on the agenda.** It's important to create written space on meeting agendas for listening and reflection. For key updates and discussion items, add "Listen to Opinions" as the next agenda item. Put listening on the agenda for group meetings and one-on-one meetings with followers.
- **Use the 1-2-4-All technique.** For important discussions, this approach will give everybody multiple opportunities to voice their views and drive toward the common purposes the team is there to pursue. It gives both naturally vocal and quiet team members equal opportunities to be heard.
- **Collect data and experiences from your stakeholders.** When you gather information about stakeholders' point of view in a systematic way, you get a more complete picture. Consider doing a listening tour, administering regular feedback surveys, or using any other thorough way of gathering data. This practice is especially important when you have too many followers to speak with individually on a regular basis.

CONCLUSION

Listening is at the heart of positive leadership. You can listen at the individual level, at the group level, and across your unit or organization. At the opening of this chapter, Melissa's fundraising experience reminds us how changing the way we listen can change how we approach our entire careers. We may be too busy talking or figuring out what to say next. We may be tempted to manage the moment to lead it in a particular conclusion. Like Melissa, this approach could very well make us miss what the other person is offering. Deep listening follows the opposite, counterintuitive impulse. Michael Schwartz, the law school dean we mentioned, explained it in this way: "The impediment to listening is [our internal] need to control."

Leadership author and speaker John Maxwell wrote, "It's one thing to communicate to people because you believe you have something of value to say. It's another to communicate with people because you believe they have value."[30] Listening shows others you value *them*. See box 7.5 to plan for your next steps. Positive leaders listen deeply to transcend differences.

Box 7.5.   **Top Takeaways**

Reflecting on your selections in the "Level 4: Put It into Practice" section, what are your top three takeaways?

1.

2.

3.

8

Inspire Unity and Effect Change

One of Alex's first jobs during his college years was delivering pizza. The thriving pizza shop employed several managers, supervisors, and shift leaders. Each individual had their own leadership style. It was also Alex's first opportunity to observe how leaders around him shaped employees' day-to-day experiences. After about six months, he could predict how well or poorly work would go by looking at who was scheduled to supervise any given shift.

"Mike" and "Gary," for example, were at opposite ends of the leadership continuum. When Gary was in charge, work felt tense and laborious. Gary was young and competent and acted professionally, but he took a relationally distant and "traditional" approach to supervision. It never felt like Gary cared to get to know anybody, and he rarely provided positive feedback. Whether the shift was busy or slow, time dragged when Gary was in charge. Everybody waited eagerly to be "cut" and go home when the shift slowed down.

In contrast, when Mike was leading, that shift was a positive experience regardless of the challenges the group faced. Like Gary, Mike was also young, competent, and professional. On top of that, Mike was a great example of a positive leader. He was consistently encouraging. He took time to get to know each team member. He made the extra effort. Not surprisingly, time passed more quickly and more enjoyably when Mike was in charge. Everybody worked extra hard and "had each other's backs" because everyone knew Mike was on their side. Like Gary and Mike, you will influence the people you lead one way or another. That's why every leader must answer for themselves: What kind of leader am I going to be? Will I do what it takes to inspire my team and effect positive change?

In this final chapter, you'll have the opportunity to prepare for the next phase of your leadership journey. You will learn the pillars and core principles needed to make deep change. You will then develop a concrete plan of action to apply what you learned and strengthen your leadership approach. Our drive-home message is this: You can't just *think* your way to better relationships and team culture. You must change what you say and do in practice.

LEVEL 1: PREPARE FOR DEEP CHANGE

Robert Quinn, professor emeritus of business at the University of Michigan, wrote, "One key to successful leadership is continuous personal change."[1] Leaders who want to create positive change, he added, must have "the courage to change themselves." Practicing positive communication is a way of creating deep change in who you are and in your organization. But we know all too well that change is not easy. We look here at two essential big-picture *pillars of leadership* that will help.

A fundamental quality of excellent leaders is continual growth.

Pillar 1: Build on Your Personal Strengths

Bruce Lee once told one of his mentees this advice: work on your strengths until they exceed your limitations.[2] As we've shown in earlier chapters, focusing on another person's strengths will increase their performance, while focusing on weaknesses usually decreases their performance. This same principle applies to your own leadership skills as well.

If you want to create deep change, we encourage you to build on your natural strengths and core values. What strengths do you have that you can keep sharpening? What do you really believe in?

One way you can discover some of your core personal values and strengths is to ask a few people you trust what they think. The people around us often see our strengths more clearly than we see them. Another way to identify your strengths is by taking a short survey offered for free online by the Institute on Character. Officially called the "VIA Survey of Character Strengths," the tool was designed to help you reflect about your natural strengths and discover your best qualities (see box 8.1). Based on this research, there are 24 possible character strengths, each tied to a larger virtue (wisdom, courage, humanity, justice, temperance, transcendence).[3] We used this survey recently in a leadership retreat and found that it hit home with participants. The experience is very affirming and may help you identify strengths you didn't realize you possessed.

For example, after taking the survey, each person was able to identify their top five character strengths: aspects of their personality that shape how they

---

Box 8.1. Identify Your Top Five Character Strengths

Instructions: Take a moment to take the "VIA Survey of Character Strengths," a tool that will identify your natural best qualities. You can take the survey at https://www.viacharacter.org. Once you have the results, you should have a ranking of those strengths, showing which are most important to you. With these strengths in mind, answer the following prompts for reflection.

- In your personal experience, how do you embody these values in your leadership approach?

- For each character strength, what is a critical story you could share to illustrate your leadership style in practice?

- What communication behaviors (and skills and techniques you have learned) naturally fit with each character strength? Make a list for each character strength.

This exercise will show who you are as a leader when you are at your best. We encourage you to share the results of the survey and your answers to these questions with some trusted friends to gain their perspectives.

think, what they do, and why they do it. Consider the differences between these two leaders, Erica and Meredith.

When Erica took the test, it revealed her top five character strengths as honesty, perspective, prudence, humor, and fairness. When the group was asked to share stories about how she embodied these character traits, the team was full of positive stories. For example, her strength in perspective, which is the "ability to see the bigger picture in life," shaped the way she worked.[4] She was excellent at putting difficult conversations in a larger context, including the past, present, and future of the organization. Her team members noted that she was great at asking questions and often asked people to consider the implications of the decision being made: "Have you thought about how this would affect our new employees?" Her strength in perspective also helped her stay true to her belief that she should put her family first.

Similarly, the team reflected on Meredith's top five strengths: humor, love of learning, curiosity, creativity, and appreciation of beauty and excellence. It was easy to notice, for instance, that Meredith often joked in the middle of the meeting, poked at her colleagues to get a reaction, and was often the first one to laugh. But the group also picked up on her strength of creativity. This character trait led her to effectively respond to challenges. She exhibited a natural willingness to try new things and encouraged her team to do the same in a safe environment. She asked questions and was open to alternative thinking.

You'll notice that Erica's and Meredith's strengths only overlapped on *humor*. The remaining four strengths were unique to each of them. Your results will likely show additional strengths that neither Erica nor Meredith possess. That's expected. Each individual builds on their own signature mixture of strengths.

If you align your character strengths with the positive communication behaviors you have learned, you will tap into a world of opportunities for you as a leader. You will keep building on your strengths, and ultimately, as Bruce Lee put it, they will outweigh your weaknesses. Once you know your core values and your strengths, you will need purpose to move forward.

Pillar 2: Develop Your Purpose

Deep personal change requires a greater sense of purpose. What motivates us and others is knowing where we are going and having a direction toward something greater than ourselves. As you know well, every great leader needs a compelling vision. As authors Quinn and Spreitzer explained, developing big purpose-driven goals means "envisioning future achievements" that trigger "a shift in attention from actuality to possibility."[5]

In their research on deep change and personal transformation, Robert and Ryan Quinn explained that leaders can immediately tap into their sense of purpose by answering some fundamental questions to guide them. These questions include the following: "What result do I want to create?" or "What goal would be the most challenging and engaging?"[6] Using these questions and the exercise we developed in box 8.2, you can develop a sense of what you really want to accomplish and use that energy to move yourself and the organization forward.

Box 8.2. **Find Your Purpose**

Instructions: Take a moment to answer the following three fundamental questions about where you and your team are headed together. Use the questions to dream big about how you can apply what you have learned in this book to take you and your organization to the next level.

- Using the power of positive communication, what result do I really want to create for myself and for my organization? *Notes:*

- Based on the reading in this book, what goal would be the most challenging and engaging for me to take on? *Notes:*

- As a leader, "What would be the most ambitious and exciting goal I could pursue?" *Notes:*

In his famous book *Man's Search for Meaning,* Viktor Frankl showed that a person could overcome any hardship if there was something for them to live for. "Life," he wrote, "is never made unbearable by circumstances, but only by lack of meaning and purpose."[7] With purpose, you too can respond to the challenges, dilemmas, and difficulties that naturally arise in organizational leadership.

Becoming a great leader requires reflection, depth, and vision. You've now identified your strengths and found your purpose. You've got energizing goals and know how to tap into the power of positive communication. Still, you'll need to avoid daily traps and misconceptions so that you can stay true and consistent to your vision. That's what we focus on next.

LEVEL 2: STICK WITH TRIED-AND-TRUE PRINCIPLES

In seminars and workshops on positive communication, people often ask questions that anticipate discouraging results when they picture putting positive communication skills into practice. In a webinar Julien conducted, for example, one person asked, "How do you deal with people who get adversarial once you communicate in a truthful/honest way with them?" Another chimed in and asked: "With some people, even if we listen deeply, they do not. How do you communicate with such people?" A third posed this question: "How do you ask open questions and get quick resolution?"

When we hear questions like these, we find ourselves empathizing. Yes, communicating well is challenging. Unfortunately, no magic potion exists that will solve all leadership challenges. Still, our fundamental belief is that practicing the six central positive practices you've learned in this book will help in *most* situations. The trouble is that the communication process is often fraught with misconceptions and traps that can discourage us. Most of us also respond to others with our *automatic response system*—we draw on our personal experiences, our past, our pains, and our hopes, and we may even have a hard time sticking to what we know works. In this section, we offer four principles to help you clarify your thinking, stay motivated, and lean into the power of positive communication. Before you transition, see box 8.3 to test your misconceptions.

Box 8.3. **Check Your Misconceptions**

Instructions: Take a moment to check your misconceptions about positive communication. Read each statement and decide whether you agree or disagree with it.

True or False   I can *fake* my way through relationships with the right behaviors.

True or False   Positive communication will fix strained relationships *quickly*.

True or False   Communicating positively is mainly about accomplishing *my* goals.

True or False   Positive communication skills should be followed *exactly* as specified in this book.

Note: If you answered "true" to any of these statements, you will experience a significant lack of motivation (and setback) when trying to put what you've learned into practice. As you'll see later, the "correct" answer to these statements is false.

Principle 1: Embrace Your Authenticity

One of the most popular misconceptions leaders have about positive communication is that they need to somehow fake their way through relationships and can use positive communication to trick people into feeling valued and cared for. That's not our position.

Your leadership style and your communication behaviors must be genuine. The one common denominator across all professionals and leaders we interviewed is that they practice positive leadership authentically. Remember what our friend and mentor Rob Ulmer said about working with people, "You have to be interested in who they are and what they're about. You have to care." The practices outlined in the book aren't meant to be mere surface-level behaviors you perform to impress others or to get by. People will see right through that. You need to genuinely like people and want to engage with them. Be a living example of the values you expect of others.

At the same time, you will not always be in a naturally sunny mood or feel like being a positive force. In the midst of pressure, anxiety, and even crises, you will need to choose the high road and rely on the compass you've adopted in this book. When the heat is on, take a moment to double-check your beneath-the-surface attitude. Remind yourself that you are committed to giving your people your best. Make sure your heart is in it and follow through with the behaviors you have learned.

Be a living example of the values you expect of others.

Principle 2: Take a Long-Term Perspective

A second common misconception is that strained relationships or hostile environments can be fixed quickly. Obviously one simple action can break trust between people, but it takes much more work to build trust and maintain it.

Leading with a relationship-centered approach is a long-term investment, not a shortcut solution. Some followers will respond well almost right away. Be grateful for those moments. Others may take quite a long time to come around. Some will never respond in kind. That's okay. Positive leadership creates an opportunity, an open door other people can choose to walk through.

Tied to this misconception is the thinking that we can somehow control how others will respond. A positive communication approach is not designed to control others. The main thing you can do in leadership is develop your skills and help to create an environment for connection. In a recent leadership seminar we led, a group of executive leaders reflected on what it took to facilitate deep change in an organization. Through our exercises and discussion, they realized that all positive change relied on similar processes. They found that in their experience, deep change occurs when leaders:

√ build a safe environment,
√ engage in healthy dialogue,
√ avoid making assumptions about others and are open to others,
√ provide space for personal and professional growth,
√ provide and offer support, and
√ share in failures and learn with and from others.

Culture change is made possible by your actions. Positive communication is always first and foremost *a process*.

Positive leadership is a marathon, not a sprint.

We also invite you to be patient with yourself. As mentioned in the opening chapter, what you've learned in this book is not superficial leadership. We are not offering "hacks," "tricks," or "quick fixes." Positive leadership is a marathon, not a sprint. When you start putting positive communication principles into practice, some techniques won't feel 100 percent natural, especially at first. Initial discomfort or lack of fluency is common for virtually all new skills. If you have ever taken a dance class, studied martial arts, or learned to drive a new type of vehicle, this awkward phase will feel familiar. Positive communication skills are no different. Trust the research. Trust the process. As John Maxwell once said, "Everything worthwhile in life is uphill."[8] The more you put these skills into practice, the more natural you will feel over time. The more you adopt a positive communication mindset, the more opportunities you will see to lead with positive approaches. It's critical to take a long-term view to see the full benefits of walking this path.

When you face obstacles in the road, stick to your compass and what you believe in. If you find yourself slipping back into old habits, shake it off and find a way to adapt, recalibrate, and get back on track. Great leaders celebrate every personal forward step they make. Take time to look back to see how far you've come. Find ways to pause to recognize and mark any progress on the path. This will help you see that positive communication is a journey, not a destination.

Principle 3: Meet the Needs of Your People

Third, leaders applying positive communication often assume that the work is all about reaching their goals. "If I practice positive communication," they think, "I can get what I want and accomplish *my* goals." Positive leadership is not a self-centered approach; it is about using the power of communication to meet the needs of your most critical stakeholders.

You must build relationships and use positive leadership practices for the benefit of the people you are leading. Rest assured, when you put your people first, your own leadership will flourish. This is a lesson Wegman's Food

Markets lives by that has propelled the company to the top of *Fortune* magazine's "Best Places to Work" list for over a decade.

If you've never shopped there, Wegman's is a popular family-owned supermarket chain in the northeastern region of the United States. It's known
for an incredible selection and even more outstanding customer experience.
By all measures, Wegman's is an aspirational role model organization in the
supermarket industry because of how well the company treats its employees.

Although many less successful companies still preach some version of the
outdated motto "The customer comes first," Wegman's takes a counterintuitive approach: "the *employee* comes first." Wegman's leaders learned long
ago that putting their employees first was a much more effective long-term
commitment. As a result of this philosophy, Wegman's employees then treat
each other and their customers exceptionally well. The company's entire
leadership philosophy centers on the good the organization creates for others.
In the same way, we believe when leaders make positive investments in their
people, everybody wins.

Principle 4: Adapt These Principles to Make Them Work for You

The final misconception occurs when people think about positive communication with a fixed, black-and-white mindset. We once worked with
a leader for several months on their communication skills. In reflecting on
their learning experience, they said: "I finally realized that communicating
well is not just about following a set of rules. It's about being flexible and
drawing on the knowledge that I have to make a positive difference." They
said, "this experience made my mind grayer."

You've learned positive leadership principles and practices in this book.
The "Wheel of Positive Communication" is a guide for action, not a set of
laws. Relationships are too complex to be boiled down to one-size-fits-all
behaviors that work in all situations. Although the underlying principles
are universal, the way these communication practices look and sound differ
across settings. Each workplace is unique and has its own unspoken norms,
expectations, and culture. Use your best judgment in adapting the lessons
in the book to your professional context. As the best-selling author Paulo
Coelho wrote, "The best way to prepare for a challenge is to cultivate the
ability to draw on an infinite variety of responses."[9]

You must also adapt what you've learned to fit your unique personality, the strengths you identified earlier in the chapter, and the specific circumstances you face. Whether you are introverted or extroverted, for instance, you will need to adapt the lessons from this book. Whether you bond with others easily or take a more reserved approach, you can still use positive communication skills in ways that fit your strengths. The general intention of the model is to move in the direction of others, to open a space for interaction and connection, and to build more compassionate and generous relationships. That will surely require you to adapt your approach to make the model work for you.

You have the skills, the techniques, and the strategies to practice positive communication in your leadership approach. You have a sense now of how to fight common misconceptions, as summarized in box 8.4. Now, it's time to plan for your next steps.

Box 8.4. Fight Your Misconceptions Summary

As you engage in positive communication, stick to our core principles:

- ✓ Embrace Authenticity and Trust the Process
- ✓ Take a Long-Term Perspective and Have Faith in the Work
- ✓ Focus on Meeting the Needs of Your People
- ✓ Adapt to New Situations and Contexts and Develop a Range of Responses

---

LEVEL 3: MAKE A PLAN

Julien recently lead a two-day leadership retreat for a group of senior executives for a large global organization. The focus of the retreat was to create group cohesiveness, enhance engagement, help the team embody newly developed values and principles, and take action. The team was working exceptionally well throughout the retreat. They developed a compelling mission statement and identified core values they believed in. But, as soon as the discussion moved to action and concrete commitments, the group stalled. One of the group members noticed the pattern and spoke up: "If we do not have any concrete actions that we are going to commit to, then all we have are words on paper. It's a great exercise, but this is what we've done in this company for years." He said again, "Just words on paper. If we do not have action items, commitments, and accountability, this work will mean nothing." This statement was exactly what people needed to hear. After it, they hunkered down in the conversation and outlined concrete action steps that they committed to immediately.

We want the same for you. As the New York pastor Peter Marshall once said, "Small deeds done are better than great deeds planned." Plans don't have to be perfect. They just have to be implemented. Both research and practice have shown the impact the practices in the "Wheel of Positive Communication" can have on your team and in your organization. Follow these easy steps to transform the behaviors you have learned into an ingrained leadership habit:

STEP 1   Start by revisiting the end of each chapter. Select *one key takeaway* from the end of each chapter that you want to put into practice in a concrete way next week. Write down in the space below each key takeaway you have chosen.

Chapter 2:

Chapter 3:

Chapter 4:

Chapter 5:

Chapter 6:

Chapter 7:

STEP 2 Now, take a moment to reflect about each takeaway and decide how you will enact it in a specific leadership situation. Here we are asking you to consider the actual event, the person(s) with whom you will be communicating, and when this conversation/initiative will occur. Think of this as being intentional: "This is what I'm going to do in this situation." To guide your reflection, consider this sample plan:

Communication	Who	What	When
CREATE Greet to create human contact	John	Stop by the office to say hello with warmth and check to see how he is doing.	Monday morning
DISCOVER Ask to discover the unknown	Team	Start team meeting with a question: "Who is one of your most inspirational heroes?"	Opening of meeting on Tuesday
AFFECT Compliment to affect people's sense of self	Constance	Offer a compliment on a recent presentation: "You've really improved your public speaking. You delivered a memorable message on Friday."	One-on-one meeting on Wednesday
DEEPEN Disclose to deepen relationships	Team	Share with leadership team two shortcomings that I'm planning to work on.	Meeting on Tuesday
GIVE Encourage to give support	Stan	Offer support because he didn't get a promotion. Help put his professional setback into a big-picture context.	One-on-one meeting on Thursday
TRANSCEND Listen to transcend differences	Team	Spend 80% of the meeting listening carefully.	Friday's special feedback meeting

STEP 3 Using the sample plan we have provided as inspiration, fill in the following blank table with your own goals and initiatives that are tailored specifically to your goals, your team, and your organization:

Communication	Who	What	When
CREATE Greet to create human contact			
DISCOVER Ask to discover the unknown			
AFFECT Compliment to affect people's sense of self			
DEEPEN Disclose to deepen relationships			
GIVE Encourage to give support			
TRANSCEND Listen to transcend differences			

Your approach to leadership is a daily choice. We encourage you to commit and put your communication plan into practice this coming week. Make it your goal to turn these six positive communication skills into habits. Then continue putting these and the other positive communication skills you've learned into practice each and every day for the foreseeable future.

The more you practice these skills, the more you'll notice that the small changes, "tweaks," and subtle improvements you make can have a big positive impact. You'll take yourself from the fundamentals to more advanced applications of the six core skills. In time, the cycle of positive change and transformation will be in full swing.

> **"Excellence, then, is not an action, but a habit."**
>
> **—Aristotle**

Richard Williams, father of the famed tennis stars Serena and Venus Williams, started their tennis journey with a clear plan. Before he started training each of them on the tennis court, he wrote a 78-page document outlining every step of his dream for his daughters and the ways in which he would accomplish those steps. Then, at every practice he made a sign with his favorite motto to inspire his daughters. The motto was this: "When you fail to plan, you plan to fail." By comparison, the plan you've drafted here is much more straightforward. It's a plan that charts the first steps on your renewed leadership journey. And after you've taken the first several steps, just keep putting one foot in front of the other.

CONCLUSION

Alex's former pizza place supervisor, Mike, was and still is an exemplary leader. For decades, Mike has led hundreds of employees on dozens of successful teams across various businesses. He's treated people like gold all the while. Alex still catches up with him via calls or texts a few times each year and is fortunate to count him as a friend. When it comes to his leadership approach, Mike realized early in his career that his team members saw him as a role model for their own behavior. In a recent conversation, Mike said humbly, "Through trial and error, I learned the hard way that when you treat people well, people will treat you well. When people don't feel respected, you'll be fighting that battle every waking hour of your existence. And they'll soon be looking for another opportunity elsewhere where they do feel appreciated. You have to be willing to give them your best before you expect to get their best. And you won't get their best *until* you do."

You now have the knowledge, skills, and tools to be a leader who will inspire unity and effect real change. But unless you take the next step and practice positive communication in your own life, this book will be "just words on paper." If you make a change in the way you interact with others, you will create a revolution in who you are. You will create a revolution in your relationships with others and lead the way to creating a positive workplace environment for all. And that's positive communication and leadership in action.

Acknowledgments

Writing a book is always a collective enterprise, and we are grateful for the many contributions of our family, friends, and colleagues along the way. We are especially grateful for the opportunity provided by Rowman & Littlefield and our wonderful editor Natalie Mandziuk and her production team. We are thankful to the anonymous reviewers who provided excellent feedback to strengthen the original manuscript. We also want to take a moment to thank the positive leaders we interviewed for this book, including Robert Ulmer, Pete Tanguay, Julie Allison, Mahendra Lohani, Allen Weiner, Anne Ricketts, Hollie Packman, Kristen Eichhorn, and Stan Deetz. In each interview we conducted, we learned nuggets of wisdom and felt inspired by the firm belief each person had in the power of human communication in leadership. We are also each grateful for the opportunity to work together and how writing this book helped reconnect us and strengthen us as friends and colleagues.

Julien's Personal Acknowledgment

I have had the pleasure of working with great leaders and mentors throughout my career. To this day, I am still in awe of the impact that those individuals have had on me. I am especially indebted to my undergraduate mentors at the University of Northern Iowa, Marvin Jensen and my friend Bill, both of whom inspired me to love the study of communication. As a graduate student, I was fortunate to work with Karen Tracy, who taught me the value of paying close attention to discourse with the impulse to solve real problems. I also want to extend a word of gratitude to Robert Ulmer and Lisa Bond-Maupin, who showed me how to lead effectively and positively. I am fortunate to work with a group of colleagues in my home department who are supportive, encouraging, and all-around inspiring: April Chatham-Carpenter, Avinash Thombre, Gerald Driskill, Carol Thompson, Kristen McIntyre, Bailey Oliver-Blackburn, and Katie Halford. Finally, I am so grateful for my family and friends. Thank you also to my wife Meg for being a pillar of our family, for your love, and for your constant support. Without you, none of this would be possible. To my kids, Hugo, John Luke, and Claire, you give me joy and happiness—thank you *mes amours*.

Alex's Personal Acknowledgement

Like Julien, I've been very fortunate to work with some amazing and inspiring leaders, supervisors, and mentors over the years. Their lasting influence on my life was one of my main motivations for writing this book. I want to acknowledge the positive influence Robert Ulmer had on my early teaching career and his continued support. Like him, many of the other leaders we talked to while writing this book—Allen Weiner, Kristen Eichhorn, Hollie Packman, Stan Deetz, and "Mike" (chapter 8)—are just a small sample of the positive leaders I "came up" under. I'm also grateful for my supportive departmental colleagues and leaders at SUNY Brockport, who supported my sabbatical to write this book. Finally, I'm grateful to God, Erin, and Soren for the amazing life I enjoy.

Notes

PREFACE

1. Begley, E. (2022, December 13). World Cup 2022: Antoine Griezmann—an underrated France legend? *BBC Sport*. https://www.bbc.com/sport/football/63934955.amp

2. Flynn, J. (2022, October 16). 25 trending remote work statistics [2022]: Facts, trends, and projections. *Zippia.com*. https://www.zippia.com/advice/remote-work-statistics/

3. Hernandez, A. (2022, December 14). World Cup 2022: Didier Deschamps, the starting XI, and the happy substitutes. *LeMonde*. https://www.lemonde.fr/en/world-cup-2022/article/2022/12/14/world-cup-2022-didier-deschamps-the-starting-xi-and-the-happy-substitutes_6007748_209.html

CHAPTER 1

1. Dutton, J. E., Glynn, M. A., & Spreitzer, G. (2008). Positive organizational scholarship. In J. Barling & C. L. Cooper (Eds.), *The SAGE handbook of organizational behavior* (Vol. 1, pp. 693–712). SAGE; Cameron K., & Spreitzer, G. M. (eds.). (2012). *Oxford handbook of positive organizational scholarship*. Oxford University Press; Cameron, K., Dutton, J., & Quinn, R. E. (Eds.). (2003). *Positive organizational scholarship: Foundations of a new discipline*. Berrett-Koehler; and Quinn, R. E. (1996). *Deep change: Discovering the leader within*. Jossey-Bass.

2. Cameron, K. (2012). *Positive leadership: Strategies for extraordinary performance*. Berrett-Koehler.

3. Cameron, K. (2012). *Positive leadership: Strategies for extraordinary performance.* Berrett-Koehler.

4. Spreitzer, G. M., & Sonenshein, S. (2003). Positive deviance and extraordinary organizing. In K. Cameron, J. Dutton, & R. Quinn (Eds.), *Positive organizational scholarship* (pp. 207–224). Berrett-Koehler.

5. Cameron, K. (2012). *Positive leadership: Strategies for extraordinary performance.* Berrett-Koehler.

6. Bartlett, R. C., & Collins, S. D. (2011). *Aristotle's nicomachean ethics.* University of Chicago Press.

7. Cameron, K. (2012). *Positive leadership: Strategies for extraordinary performance.* Berrett-Koehler.

8. Dutton, J. E. (2003). *Energize your workplace: How to create and sustain high-quality connections at work.* John Wiley & Sons; and Dutton, J. E., & Heaphy, E. D. (2003). The power of high-quality connections. In K. Cameron, J. E. Dutton, & R. E. Quinn (Eds.), *Positive organizational scholarship* (pp. 263–278). Berrett-Koehler.

9. Biganeh, M., & Young, S. L. (2021). Followers' perceptions of positive communication practices in leadership: What matters and surprisingly what does not. *International Journal of Business Communication.* https://doi.org/10.1177%2F2329488420987277

10. Dutton, J. E., Workman, K. M., & Hardin, A. E. (2014). Compassion at work. *Annual Review of Organic Psychology & Organic Behavior, 1*, 277–304.

11. Cameron, K. (2012). *Positive leadership: Strategies for extraordinary performance.* Berrett-Koehler.

12. Mirivel, J. C. (2014). *The art of positive communication: Theory and practice.* Peter Lang; Mirivel, J. C. (2017). *How communication scholars think and act: A lifespan perspective.* Peter Lang; and Mirivel, J. (2019). On the nature of peak communication: Communication behaviors that make a difference on well-being and happiness. In J. A. M. Velázquez & C. Pulido (Eds.), *The Routledge handbook of positive communication: Contributions of an emerging community of research on communication for happiness and social change* (pp. 50–59). Routledge.

13. Mirivel, J. C. (2014). *The art of positive communication: Theory and practice.* Peter Lang.

14. Mirivel, J. C., & Oliver-Blackburn, B. (forthcoming). How positive communication creates peak communication moments. In C. L. Fisher, C. Fowler, C. J. Krieger, M. Pitts, A. Worthington, & J. Nussbaum (Eds.), *Health communication, language, and social action: Across the life span.* Peter Lang.

15. Biganeh, M., & Young, S. L. (2021). Followers' perceptions of positive communication practices in leadership: What matters and surprisingly what does not. *International Journal of Business Communication.* https://doi.org/10.1177%2F2329488420987277

16. Biganeh, M., & Young, S. L. (2021). Followers' perceptions of positive communication practices in leadership: What matters and surprisingly

what does not. *International Journal of Business Communication.* https://doi.org /10.1177%2F2329488420987277

17. Biganeh, M., & Young, S. L. (2021). Followers' perceptions of positive communication practices in leadership: What matters and surprisingly what does not. *International Journal of Business Communication.* https://doi.org/10.1177 %2F2329488420987277

CHAPTER 2

1. Bernstein-Yamashiro, B. (2004). Learning relationships: Teacher-student connections, learning, and identity in high school. *New Directions for Youth Development, 103,* 55–70; and Weinstein, L., Laverghetta, A., Alexander, R., & Stewart, M. (2009). Teacher greetings increase college students' test scores. *College Student Journal, 43,* 452–454..

2. Singhal, A. (2013). Transforming education from the inside-out: Positive deviance to enhance learning and student retention. In R. Hiemstra and P. Carré (Eds.), *International perspectives on adult learning* (pp. 12–34). Information Age Publishing.

3. Comstock, L. M., Hooper, E. M., Goodwin, J. M., & Goodwin, J. S. (1982). Physician behaviors that correlate with patient satisfaction. *Journal of Medical Education, 57,* 105–112.

4. Johnson, R. A., Houmanfar, R., & Smith, G. S. (2010). The effect of implicit and explicit rules on customer greeting and productivity in a retail organization. *Journal of Organizational Behavior Management, 30,* 38–48.

5. Gordon, J. (2017). *The power of positive leadership: How and why positive leaders transform teams and organizations and change the world.* John Wiley & Sons.

6. Wingfield, D. (2011). *An investigation of the effect of communication education on Ethnocentrism* [Master's thesis]. University of Arkansas at Little Rock; Wingfield, D., & Mirivel, J. C. (2011). *We are more similar than different: An assessment of the impact of communication training on Pakistani students' cultural mindsets* [Paper presentation]. National Communication Association Annual Meeting, New Orleans, LA.

7. Holmes, J., & Stubbe, M. (2013). *Power and politeness in the workplace.* Routledge.

8. Holmes, J. (2000). Doing collegiality and keeping control at work: Small talk in government departments. In J. Coupland (Ed.), *Small talk* (pp. 32–61). Routledge; and Holmes, J. (2003). Small talk at work: Potential problems for workers with an intellectual disability. *Research on Language and Social Interaction, 36,* 65–84.

9. Vaillant, G. E. (2012). *Triumphs of experience: The men of the Harvard grant study.* Harvard University Press.

10. Shenk, J. W. (2009, June). What makes us happy. *The Atlantic.*

11. Holmes, J. (2000). Doing collegiality and keeping control at work: Small talk in government departments. In J. Coupland (Ed.), *Small talk* (pp. 32–61). Routledge; and Holmes, J. (2003). Small talk at work: Potential problems for workers with an intellectual disability. *Research on Language and Social Interaction, 36*, 65–84. https://doi.org/10.1207/S15327973RLSI3601_4

12. Waldvogel, J. (2002). Some features of workplace emails. *New Zealand English Journal, 16*, 42–52.

13. Waldvogel, J. (2007). Greetings and closings in workplace email. *Journal of Computer-Mediated Communication, 12*, 456–477.

14. Waldvogel, J. (2007). Greetings and closings in workplace email. *Journal of Computer-Mediated Communication, 12*, 456–477.

15. Craig, R. T. (1999). Communication theory as a field. *Communication Theory, 9*(2), 119–161.

16. Morin, A. (2018, June 26). *Top 25 tactics of workplace bullies.* Inc.com. https://www.inc.com/amy-morin/top-25-tactics-of-workplace-bullies-in-order-of-most-to-least-popular.html

17. Paymar, J. (2012, February 2). Speak like a leader. *Forbes.* https://www.forbes.com/sites/jimpaymar/2012/02/02/speak-like-a-leader/?sh=47640c157144

18. Mckinney, E. H., Jr., Barker, J. R., Davis, K. J., & Smith, D. (2005). How swift starting action teams get off the ground: What United flight 232 and airline flight crews can tell us about team communication. *Management Communication Quarterly, 19*, 198–237.

CHAPTER 3

1. Maxwell, J. C. (2014). *Good leaders ask great questions: Your foundation for successful leadership.* Hachette, UK.

2. Trent, Tererai. (2015, November). *Forgotten women and girls* [Video]. TED conferences. https://www.youtube.com/watch?v=2n2DXFhwTE4&t=1s. Sivaram, V. (2020, October). *India's historic opportunity to industrialize using clean energy* [Video]. TED Conferences. https://youtu.be/2n2DXFhwTE4

3. Goldsmith, M. (2007, November 18). Is the role of a leader changing? *Harvard Business Review.* https://hbr.org/2007/11/is-the-role-of-a-leader-changi

4. Sacks, H. (1992). *Lectures on conversation* (Vol. I). Blackwell.

5. Bales, R. F. (1950). A set of categories for the analysis of small group interaction. *American Sociological Review, 15*, 257–263.

6. Goldsmith, M., & Morgan, H. 2004. Leadership is a contact sport: The "follow-up factor" in management development. *Strategy and Business, 36*, 71–79.

7. Wodak, R., Kwon, W., & Clarke, I. (2011). "Getting people on board": Discursive leadership for consensus building in team meetings. *Discourse & Society, 22*, 592–644.

8. Bechler, C., & Johnson, S. D. (1995). Leadership and listening: A study of member perceptions. *Small Group Research, 26*, 77–85; and Johnson, S. D., & Bechler, C. (1998). Examining the relationship between listening effectiveness and leadership emergence: Perceptions, behaviors, and recall. *Small Group Research, 29*, 452–471.

9. Van Quaquebeke, N., & Felps, W. (2018). Respectful inquiry: A motivational account of leading through asking questions and listening. *Academy of Management Review, 43*, 5–27.

10. Chesebro, J. L. (2014). *Professional communication at work: Interpersonal strategies for career success*. Routledge.

11. Anonymous. (2021, November 16). The benefits of asking questions and really listening. *AOM Insights*. https://journals.aom.org/doi/abs/10.5465/amr.2014.0537.summary; and Van Quaquebeke, N., & Felps, W. (2018). Respectful inquiry: A motivational account of leading through asking questions and listening. *Academy of Management Review, 43*, 5–27.

12. Singhal, A. (2006). *The practice of medicine is in the interactions: A day with Robert A. Lindberg*. The Plexus Institute. http://www.innovationlabs.com/summit/discovery1/reading_materials/Lindberg-Medcine%20in%20the%20Interactions-Singhal.pdf. The following quotes about Dr. Lindberg are all from this source.

13. Brümmer, K. (2016, September 21). Questions motivate: Respectful Inquiry study explores theory behind the leadership technique. Informationsdienst Wissenschaft (Scientific Information Service). https://idw-online.de/en/aboutus

14. Maxwell, J. (2014, August 19). *Questions to ask during a learning session*. https://www.johnmaxwell.com/blog/questions-to-ask-during-a-learning-session/

15. Hensel, A. (2017, February 14). The 1 incredibly detailed job interview question Elon Musk always asks. *Inc*. https://www.inc.com/magazine/202210/tim-crino/nebia-moen-quattro-green-growth-2022.html

16. Lyon, A. (2017). *Case studies in courageous organizational communication: Research and practice for effective workplaces*. Peter Lang.

17. Manciagli, D. (2017). 5 ways to provide the optimal employee workplace experience. *The Business Journals*. https://www.bizjournals.com/bizjournals/how-to/human-resources/2017/02/5-ways-to-provide-the-optimal-employee-workplace.html

18. Casselman, B. (2022, January 4). More quit jobs than ever, but most turnover is in low-wage work. *New York Times*. https://www.nytimes.com/2022/01/04/business/economy/job-openings-coronavirus.html

19. Dilan, E. (2022, January 3). Work-life harmony ideas to help slow the great resignation: Part 2. *Forbes*. https://www.forbes.com/sites/forbescoachescouncil/2022/01/03/work-life-harmony-ideas-to-help-slow-the-great-resignation-part-2/?sh=6815d3b76214

20. Chen, C. (2020, December 4). Shocking meeting statistics in 2021 that will take you by surprise. *Otter.Ai*. https://otter.ai/blog/meeting-statistics

21. Grenny, J., Patterson, K., McMillan, R., Switzler, A., & Gregory, E. (2012). *Crucial conversations: Tools for talking when stakes are high.* McGraw-Hill.

22. Coyle, D. (2018) *The culture code: The secrets of highly successful groups.* Bantam.

23. Shaw, G. (2020, June 18). Accentuate the positive: Appreciative inquiry as a tool for combating burnout. *NeurologyToday.* https://journals.lww.com/neuro todayonline/Fulltext/2020/06180/Accentuate_the_Positive__Appreciative_Inquiry _as_a.10.aspx

24. Cooperrider, D. L., Barrett, F., and Srivastva, S. (1995). Social construction and appreciative inquiry: A journey in organizational theory. In D. Hosking, P. Dachler, & K. Gergen (Eds.), *Management and organization: Relational alternatives to individualism* (pp. 157–200). Avebury Press.

25. Serrat, O. (2009). Asking effective questions. *Knowledge Solutions, 52,* 1–6.

26. Whitney, D., Cooperrider, D. L., Trosten-Bloom, A., & Kaplin, B. S. (2002). *Encyclopedia of positive questions: Vol. 1. Using appreciative inquiry to bring out the best in your organization.* Lakeshore Communications.

CHAPTER 4

1. Anonymous (2017, August 30). Something special about Southwest Airlines. *CBS News.* https://www.cbsnews.com/news/something-special-about-southwest -airlines/

2. Attridge, M. (2009). Measuring and managing employee work engagement: A review of the research and business literature. *Journal of Workplace Behavioral Health, 24,* 383–398; IBM. (2017). *The employee experience index: A new global measure of a human workplace and its impact.* IBM Corporation. https://www.ibm.com/down loads/cas/JDMXPMBM; Harter, J., & Adkins, A. (2015, April 8). Employees want a lot more from their managers. *Gallup.* https://www.gallup.com/workplace/236570 /employees-lot-managers.aspx; Luthans, K. (2000). Recognition: A powerful, but often overlooked, leadership tool to improve employee performance. *Journal of Leadership Studies, 7,* 31–39; and Brun, J. P., & Dugas, N. (2008). An analysis of employee recognition: Perspectives on human resources practices. *The International Journal of Human Resource Management, 19*(4), 716–730.

3. Goffman, E. (1990). *The presentation of self in everyday life.* Penguin.

4. Knapp, M. L., Stohl, C., & Reardon, K. (1981). Memorable messages. *Journal of Communication, 31,* 27–42.

5. Stohl, C. (1986). The role of memorable messages in the process of organizational socialization. *Communication Quarterly, 34,* 231–249.

6. Harter, J., & Adkins, A. (2015, April 8). Employees want a lot more from their managers. *Gallup.* https://www.gallup.com/workplace/236570/employees-lot-mana gers.aspx

7. Harter, J., & Adkins, A. (2015, April 8). Employees want a lot more from their managers. *Gallup*. https://www.gallup.com/workplace/236570/employees-lot-mana gers.aspx

8. IBM. (2017). *The employee experience index: A new global measure of a human workplace and its impact*. IBM Corporation.

9. IBM. (2017). *The employee experience index: A new global measure of a human workplace and its impact*. IBM Corporation.

10. Brun, J. P., & Dugas, N. (2008). An analysis of employee recognition: Perspectives on human resources practices. *The International Journal of Human Resource Management, 19*(4), 716–730; and Grawitch, M., Gottschalk, M., & David, M. (2006). The path to a healthy workplace: A critical review linking healthy workplace practices, employee well-being, and organizational improvements. *Consulting Psychology Journal: Practice and Research, 58*, 129–147.

11. Luthans, K. (2000). Recognition: A powerful, but often overlooked, leadership tool to improve employee performance. *Journal of Leadership Studies, 7*, 31–39.

12. Luna, T., & Renninger, L. (2021). *The leader lab: Core skills to become a great manager faster*. Wiley & Sons; and Renninger, L. (2020, February 20). *The secret to giving great feedback*. TED Conferences. https://youtu.be/wtl5UrrgU8c

13. Cameron, K. (2012). *Positive leadership: Strategies for extraordinary performance*. Berrett-Koehler.

14. Boothby, E., Zhao, X., & Bohns, V. K. (2021, February 24). A simple compliment can make a big difference. *Harvard Business Review*. https://hbr.org/2021/02/a -simple-compliment-can-make-a-big-difference. All quotes in this paragraph are from this source.

15. Kumar, V., & Pansari, A. (2015). Measuring the benefits of employee engagement. *MIT Sloan Management Review, 56*(4), 67.

16. Abraham, S. (2012). Job satisfaction as an antecedent to employee engagement. *SIES Journal of Management, 8*, 27–36.

17. Harter, J. K., Schmidt, F. L., & Keyes, C. L. (2002). Well-being in the workplace and its relationship to business outcomes: A review of the Gallup Studies. In C. L. Keyes & J. Haidt (Eds.), Flourishing: The positive person and the good life (pp. 205–224). American Psychological Association.

18. Attridge, M. (2009). Measuring and managing employee work engagement: A review of the research and business literature. *Journal of Workplace Behavioral Health, 24*, 383–398.

19. Kumar, V., & Pansari, A. (2015). Measuring the benefits of employee engagement. *MIT Sloan Management Review, 56*(4), 67.

20. Luthans, K. (2000). Recognition: A powerful, but often overlooked, leadership tool to improve employee performance. *Journal of Leadership Studies, 7*, 31–39.

21. Daniel, T. A., & Metcalf, G. S. (2005). The fundamentals of employee recognition. *Society of Human Resource Management, 1*, 7.

22. Luthans, K. (2000). Recognition: A powerful, but often overlooked, leadership tool to improve employee performance. *Journal of Leadership Studies, 7*, 31–39.

CHAPTER 5

1. Mirivel, J. C. (2017). *How communication scholars think and act.* Peter Lang Publishing.

2. Gumpert, D. E., & Boyd, P. D. (1984). The loneliness of the small business owner. *Harvard Business Review, 62,* 24; and Bell, R. A., Roloff, M. E., Van Camp, K., & Karol, S. H. (1990). Is it lonely at the top? Career success and personal relationships. *Journal of Communication, 40,* 9–23.

3. Rokach, A. (2014). Leadership and loneliness. *International Journal of Leadership and Change, 2,* 48–58.

4. Blackwell, J. (2022, January 11). Nick Saban defends Bryce Young and Will Anderson: They're not defined by one game. *Bama Central.* https://www .si.com/college/alabama/bamacentral/nick-saban-defends-bryce-young-and-will-an derson-theyre-not-defined-by-one-game-blackwell#:~:text=%22These%20two%20 guys%20sitting%20up,not%20be%20here%20without%20them

5. Brown, B. (2013). *Daring greatly: How the courage to be vulnerable transforms the way we live, love, parent and lead.* Portfolio Penguin.

6. Du Prè, A. (2002). Accomplishing the impossible: Talking about body and soul and mind during a medical visit. *Health Communication, 14,* 1–21.

7. Cayanus, J. L. (2004). Effective instructional practice: Using teacher self-disclosure as an instructional tool. *Communication Teacher, 18,* 6–9.

8. Emmerich, A. I., Knoll, M., & Rigotti, T. (2020). The authenticity of the others: How teammates' authenticity relates to our well-being. *Small Group Research, 51,* 175–207.

9. Emmerich, A. I., Knoll, M., & Rigotti, T. (2020). The authenticity of the others: How teammates' authenticity relates to our well-being. *Small Group Research, 51,* 175–207.

10. Weiner, A. N. (2006). *So smart but . . .: How intelligent people lose credibility and how they can get it back.* John Wiley & Sons.

11. Rogers, C. R. (1961). *On becoming a person: A therapist's view of psychotherapy.* Houghton Mifflin.

12. Grenny, J., Patterson, K., McMillan, R., Switzler, A., & Gregory, E. (2012). *Crucial conversations: Tools for talking when stakes are high.* McGraw-Hill.

13. Comte-Sponville, A. (2001). *A small treatise on the great virtues* (C. Temerson, Trans.). Metropolitan Books.

14. Davis, D. E., Choe, E., Meyers, J., Wade, N., Varjas, K., Gifford, A., . . . & Worthington, E. L., Jr. (2016). Thankful for the little things: A meta-analysis of gratitude interventions. *Journal of Counseling Psychology, 63,* 20–31; and Yoshimura, S. M., & Berzins, K. (2017). Grateful experiences and expressions: The role of gratitude expressions in the link between gratitude experiences and well-being. *Review of Communication, 17,* 106–118.

15. Cameron, K. (2012). *Positive leadership: Strategies for extraordinary performance.* Berrett-Koehler.

16. Grenny, J., Patterson, K., McMillan, R., Switzler, A., & Gregory, E. (2012). *Crucial conversations: Tools for talking when stakes are high.* McGraw-Hill.

17. Lipmanowicz, H., & McCandless, K. (2014). *The surprising power of liberating structures: Simple rules to unleash a culture of innovation.* Liberating Structures Press.

18. Andersen, E. (2012, June 5). Courageous leaders don't make excuses . . .: They apologize. *Forbes.* https://www.forbes.com/sites/erikaandersen/2012/06/05/courageous-leaders-dont-make-excuses-they-apologize/?sh=83e3ff4ef8c9

19. Lyon, A. (2017). *Case studies in courageous organizational communication: Research and practice for effective workplaces.* Peter Lang.

20. Jones, D. (2019, May 30). Aflac CEO Dan Amos knows the key to lasting 30 years. *Investor's Business Daily.* https://www.investors.com/news/management/leaders-and-success/aflac-ceo-dan-amos-shares-secret-lasting-30-years/

21. Anonymous. (2020, January 30). Apollo, Challenger, Columbia lessons learned program: Interview with Mike Ciannilli. NASA Edge. https://www.nasa.gov/nasa-edge/ne1401-accllp

22. Milliken, F. J., Morrison, E. W., & Hewlin, P. F. (2003). An exploratory study of employee silence: Issues that employees don't communicate upward and why. *Journal of Management Studies, 40,* 1453–1476.

23. Bisel, R. S., Messersmith, A. S., & Kelley, K. M. (2012). Supervisor-subordinate communication: Hierarchical mum effect meets organizational learning. *The Journal of Business Communication, 49,* 128–147.

24. Weick, K. (1990). The vulnerable system: An analysis of the Tenerife air disaster. *Journal of Management, 16,* 571–593.

25. Edmondson, A. C. (2003). Speaking up in the operating room: How team leaders promote learning in interdisciplinary action teams. *Journal of Management Studies, 40*(6), 1419–1452.

26. Detert, J. R., & Burris, E. R. (2007). Leadership behavior and employee voice: Is the door really open? *Academy of Management Journal, 50*(4), 869–884.

27. Ring, D. C., Herndon, J. H., & Meyer, G. S. (2010). Case 34-2010: A 65-year-old woman with an incorrect operation on the left hand. *New England Journal of Medicine, 363,* 1950–1957.

28. Ring, D. C., Herndon, J. H., & Meyer, G. S. (2010). Case 34-2010: A 65-year-old woman with an incorrect operation on the left hand. *New England Journal of Medicine, 363,* 1950–1957.

CHAPTER 6

1. Frank, V. E. (2006). *Man's search for meaning.* Beacon Press.

2. Lynch, P. D., Eisenberger, R., & Armeli, S. (1999). Perceived organizational support: Inferior versus superior performance by wary employees. *Journal of Applied Psychology, 84,* 467–483.

3. Karasek, R. A., Triantis, K. P., & Chaudhry, S. S. (1982). Coworker and supervisor support as moderators of associations between task characteristics and mental strain. *Journal of Occupational Behaviour*, *3*(2), 181–200. https://psycnet.apa.org/doi/10.1002/job.4030030205

4. Buttigieg, S. C., & West, M. A. (2013). Senior management leadership, social support, job design and stressor-to-strain relationships in hospital practice. *Journal of Health Organization and Management*, *27*, 171–192 https://doi.org/10.1108/14777261311321761

5. Amabile, T. M., Schatzel, E. A., Moneta, G. B., & Kramer, S. J. (2004). Leader behaviors and the work environment for creativity: Perceived leader support. *The Leadership Quarterly*, *15*, 5–32.

6. Stohl, C. (1986). The role of memorable messages in the process of organizational socialization. *Communication Quarterly*, *34*, 231–249. All quotes in this paragraph are from this source.

7. Amabile, T. M., Schatzel, E. A., Moneta, G. B., & Kramer, S. J. (2004). Leader behaviors and the work environment for creativity: Perceived leader support. *The Leadership Quarterly*, *15*, 5–32.

8. Amabile, T. M., Schatzel, E. A., Moneta, G. B., & Kramer, S. J. (2004). Leader behaviors and the work environment for creativity: Perceived leader support. *The Leadership Quarterly*, *15*, 5–32.

9. Murphy, K. (2013, April 20). Opinion: Maya Angelou. *New York Times*. https://www.nytimes.com/2013/04/21/opinion/sunday/a-chat-with-maya-angelou.html

10. Mirivel, J. C. (2019). On the nature of peak communication: Communication behaviors that make a difference on well-being and happiness. In J. A. Muñiz-Velázquez & C. M. Pulido (Eds.), *The Routledge handbook of positive communication* (pp. 50–59). Routledge.

11. Holmstrom, A. J., Russell, J. C., & Clare, D. D. (2013). Esteem support messages received during the job search: A test of the CETESM. *Communication Monographs*, *80*, 220–242.

12. Maslow, M (1971). *The farther reaches of human nature*. Penguin Arkana.

13. Cranmer, G. A., Anzur, C. K., & Sollitto, M. (2017). Memorable messages of social support that former high school athletes received from their head coaches. *Communication & Sport*, *5*, 604–621. https://doi.org/10.1177%2F2167479516641934

14. Kanov, J. M., Maitlis, S., Worline, M. C., Dutton, J. E., Frost, P. J., & Lilius, J. M. (2004). Compassion in organizational life. *American Behavioral Scientist*, *47*, 808–827. https://doi.org/10.1177%2F0002764203260211

15. Hougaard, R., & Carter, J. (2022). *Compassionate leadership: How to do hard things in a human way*. Harvard University Press.

16. Klimecki, O. M., Leiberg, S., Ricard, M., & Singer, T. (2014). Differential pattern of functional brain plasticity after compassion and empathy training. *Social Cognitive and Affective Neuroscience*, *9*(6), 873–879. https://doi.org/10.1093/scan/nst060

17. Dutton, J. E., Worline, M. C., Frost, P. J., & Lilius, J. (2006). Explaining compassion organizing. *Administrative Science Quarterly, 51*, 59–96.

18. Dutton, J. E., Worline, M. C., Frost, P. J., & Lilius, J. (2006). Explaining compassion organizing. *Administrative Science Quarterly, 51*, 59–96.

19. Dutton, J. E., Worline, M. C., Frost, P. J., & Lilius, J. (2006). Explaining compassion organizing. *Administrative Science Quarterly, 51*, 59–96.

20. Dutton, J. E., Worline, M. C., Frost, P. J., & Lilius, J. (2006). Explaining compassion organizing. *Administrative Science Quarterly, 51*, 59–96.

21. Lilius, J. M., Kanov, J., Dutton, J., Worline, M. C., & Maitlis, S. (2013). *Compassion revealed.* Executive White Paper Series, Ross School of Business, University of Michigan. https://positiveorgs.bus.umich.edu/wp-content/uploads/Dutton-CompassionRevealed.pdf

22. Brownell, C. A., Zerwas, S., & Balaraman, G. (2002). Peers, cooperative play, and the development of empathy in children. *Behavioral and Brain Sciences, 25*, 28–29.

23. Dutton, J. E., Worline, M. C., Frost, P. J., & Lilius, J. (2006). Explaining compassion organizing. *Administrative Science Quarterly, 51*, 59–96; and Frankl, V. (2006). *Man's search for meaning.* Beacon Press.

24. Lilius, J. M., Worline, M. C., Dutton, J. E., Kanov, J. M., & Maitlis, S. (2011). Understanding compassion capability. *Human Relations, 64*(7), 873–899.

25. Chillakuri, B. (2020). Understanding Generation Z expectations for effective onboarding. *Journal of Organizational Change Management, 33*, 1277–1296. https://doi.org/10.1108/JOCM-02-2020-0058

26. Chillakuri, B. (2020). Understanding Generation Z expectations for effective onboarding. *Journal of Organizational Change Management, 33*, 1277–1296. https://doi.org/10.1108/JOCM-02-2020-0058

27. Ulmer, R. R., Sellnow, T. L., & Seeger, M. W. (2017). *Effective crisis communication: Moving from crisis to opportunity.* SAGE.

28. Ulmer, R. R., Sellnow, T. L., & Seeger, M. W. (2017). *Effective crisis communication: Moving from crisis to opportunity.* SAGE.

29. Kerber, R. (November 5, 2021). Aaron Feuerstein dies at 95, paid idled workers after mill fire. *Reuters.* https://www.reuters.com/world/us/aaron-feuerstein-dies-95-paid-idled-workers-after-fire-2021-11-05/

CHAPTER 7

1. Flynn, J., & Faulk, L. (2008). Listening in the workplace. *Kentucky Journal of Communication, 27*, 15–31.

2. Flynn, J., Valikoski, T. R., & Grau, J. (2008). Listening in the business context: Reviewing the state of research. *The International Journal of Listening, 22*, 141–151.

3. Mirivel, J. C. (2017). *How communication scholars think and act: A lifespan perspective.* Peter Lang.

4. Albom, M. (2009). *Have a little faith.* Simon and Schuster.

5. Brearley, L. (2015). Deep listening and leadership: An indigenous model of leadership and community development in Australia. In C. Voyageur, L. Brearley, & B. Calliou (2nd ed.), *Restoring Indigenous leadership: Wise practices in community development* (pp. 91–127). Banff Centre Press.

6. Scharmer, O. (2007). *Theory U: Leading from the future as it emerges.* Berrett-Koehler, 2009.

7. Brearley, L. (2015). Deep listening and leadership: An indigenous model of leadership and community development in Australia. In C. Voyageur, L. Brearley, & B. Calliou (2nd ed.), *Restoring Indigenous leadership: Wise practices in community development* (pp. 91–127). Banff Centre Press.

8. Brearley, L. (2015). Deep listening and leadership: An indigenous model of leadership and community development in Australia. In C. Voyageur, L. Brearley, & B. Calliou (2nd ed.), *Restoring Indigenous leadership: Wise practices in community development* (pp. 91–127). Banff Centre Press.

9. Bushe, G. R., & Marshak, R. J. (2014). The dialogic mindset in organization development. In *Research in organizational change and development* (pp. 55–97). Emerald Group Publishing. https://doi.org/10.1108/S0897-301620140000022002; and Pearce, W. B., & Pearce, K. A. (2000). Combining passions and abilities: Toward dialogic virtuosity. *Southern Journal of Communication, 65,* 161–175.

10. Cloud, H., (2013). *Boundaries for leaders.* HarperCollins.

11. Rogers, C. R. (1995). *On becoming a person: A therapist's view of psychotherapy.* Houghton Mifflin Harcourt.

12. Petersen, A. C. (2020). Empathic listening: Empowering individuals as leaders. *The Journal of Student Leadership, 3,* 63–71; and Bodie, G. D. (2011). The active-empathic listening scale (AELS): Conceptualization and evidence of validity within the interpersonal domain. *Communication Quarterly, 59*(3), 277–295.

13. Snorrason, S. K. (2014). *Exalted road of silence: How active-empathetic listening for supervisors is associated to subjective well-being and engagement among employees* [Master's thesis]. University of Iceland, School of Business, Reykjavik.

14. Mirivel, J. C. (2019). On the nature of peak communication: Communication behaviors that make a difference on well-being and happiness. In J. A. Muñiz-Velázquez & C. M. Pulido (Eds.), *The Routledge handbook of positive communication* (pp. 50–59). Routledge.

15. Rogers, C. R. (1995). *On becoming a person: A therapist's view of psychotherapy.* Houghton Mifflin Harcourt.

16. Rogers, C. R. (1995). *On becoming a person: A therapist's view of psychotherapy.* Houghton Mifflin Harcourt.

17. Covey, S. R. (2004). *The 7 habits of highly effective people: Restoring the character ethic.* Free Press.

18. Ward, A. (2014). *Civil rights brothers: The journey of Albert Porter and Allan Ward.* Stewart Creative Services.

19. Fisher, R., & Ury, W. (2011). *Getting to yes: Negotiating agreement without giving in.* Penguin Publishing.

20. Buber, M. (1970). *I and thou* (Vol. 243). Simon and Schuster.

21. Flynn, J., Valikoski, T. R., & Grau, J. (2008). Listening in the business context: Reviewing the state of research. *The International Journal of Listening*, 22, 141–151.

22. Flynn, J., Valikoski, T. R., & Grau, J. (2008). Listening in the business context: Reviewing the state of research. *The International Journal of Listening*, *22*, 141–151.

23. Lipmanowicz, H., & McCandless, K. (2014). *The surprising power of liberating structures: Simple rules to unleash a culture of innovation.* Liberating Structures Press.

24. Wolvin, A. D. (2005). Listening leadership: Hillary Clinton's listening tour. *International Journal of Listening*, *19*, 29–38.

25. Wolvin, A. D. (2005). Listening leadership: Hillary Clinton's listening tour. *International Journal of Listening*, *19*, 29–38.

26. Wolvin, A. D. (2005). Listening leadership: Hillary Clinton's listening tour. *International Journal of Listening*, *19*, 29–38.

27. Anonymous (2022). *Six keys to a successful listening tour.* https://executiveforum.com/six-keys-successful-listening/

28. Bryant, A. (2017, June 9). Chip Bergh on setting a high bar and holding people accountable. *New York Times.*

29. Secretan, L. (2006). *The art and practice of conscious leadership.* Secretan Center Inc.

30. Maxwell, John C. (2007). *The 21 irrefutable laws of leadership.* Thomas Nelson.

CHAPTER 8

1. Quinn, R. E. (1996). *Deep change: Discovering the leader within.* John Wiley & Sons.

2. Hyams, J. (1979). *Zen in the martial arts.* Bantam Books.

3. See https://www.viacharacter.org

4. Anonymous (2022, November 25). *Character strengths: Perspective.* https://www.viacharacter.org/character-strengths/perspective

5. Quinn, R. E., & Spreitzer, G. M. (2006). Entering the fundamental state of leadership: A framework for the positive transformation of self and others. In R. Burke & C. Cooper (Eds.), *Inspiring leaders* (pp. 67–83). Routledge.

6. Quinn, R. W., & Quinn, R. E. (2015). *Lift: The fundamental state of leadership.* Berrett-Koehler.

7. Frankl, V. E. (1985). *Man's search for meaning.* Simon and Schuster.

8. Maxwell, J. C. (2020). *The leader's greatest return: Attracting, developing, and multiplying leaders.* HarperCollins.

9. Coelho, P. (2012). *Aleph.* Vintage.

Index

academic departments, 107; culture of, 58–
   61; environment of, 30–31; supervisors
   of, 34–35
actions, leadership defined through, 4
active-empathic listening (AEL), 153–54
advice, 126–27, *127*, 144
AEL. *See* active-empathic listening
affirmative feedback, 76–78
Aflac (company), 112
agendas, for meetings, 165–66, 172
AI. *See* appreciative inquiry
Albom, Mitch, 151
Amare (interviewee), 155
Amos, Dan, 112
Anderson, Will, Jr., 96
Anneliese (interviewee), 129
Anzur, Christine, 129–30
apologies, 109–12, 118
appreciative inquiry (AI), 63–65, 66
April (department chairperson), 57
Arabic (language), greetings in, 16–17, *17*
Aristotle (philosopher), 189
Arvind, 149
assumptions, avoiding, 157–58
audience analysis, interactions compared
   with, 52
authenticity, behaviors reflecting, 181–82

authority structure, disclosure impacted by,
   113–14
automatic response system, 180

Balaraman, Geetha, 139
Balboa, Rocky (fictional character), 12
Barrett, Frank, 63
barriers: common, 148, 156; leadership,
   156–60, *161*; listening, 160, *161*, 164,
   171
behaviors, 115; authenticity reflected
   by, 181–82; communication, 86–87;
   communication through, 22, 30–31;
   interactions shaped by, 11; problematic,
   59; relationships impacted by, 36;
   strengths aligning with, 178; supervisors
   modeling, 189; teams inspired by, 124–
   25; virtues inspired by, 4. *See also specific
   behaviors*
Belcher, David, 75
Ben (director), 101–2
Bergh, Chip, 169–70
Best Champion Program (recognition
   program), 89–90
Biganeh, Maryam, 8, *11*
big picture, 131–32, *132*, 144, 176, 187
birth map (ice breaker), 106

207

About the Authors

Julien C. Mirivel, PhD, is professor of applied communication at the University of Arkansas at Little Rock, an author, and a professional speaker. He earned his PhD from the University of Colorado at Boulder (2005). Originally from Paris, France, he is "among the founding scholars in the emerging field of positive communication" and an award-winning teacher and scholar. In 2013, he was named a Distinguished Teaching Fellow at UA Little Rock, where he served in a number of leadership roles, including as codirector of the Academy for Teaching and Learning Excellence and chair, associate dean, and dean of the College of Social Sciences and Communication. Julien has published in the most rigorous journals in the field of communication and is the author of two books on positive communication: *The Art of Positive Communication: Theory and Practice* and *How Communication Scholars Think and Act: A Lifespan Perspective*. Dr. Mirivel has delivered hundreds of keynotes, trainings, and workshops on how to communicate effectively. He is a TEDx speaker whose mission is to inspire individuals and groups to communicate more positively at work and at home. He is founder of the Positive Communication Network, whose mission is to foster a community dedicated to creating better social worlds for all through positive communication research, education, and practice. For more information and resources, please visit julienmirivel.com.

Alexander Lyon, PhD, is a professor of communication at SUNY Brockport, an author, a consultant, and a speaker. He graduated with a PhD in communication from the University of Colorado, Boulder (2003). His teaching focuses mainly on communication in the workplace and leadership. His first book, *Courageous Organizational Communication Case Studies*, looks at both inspirational workplaces and cautionary tales. He has published original research in peer-reviewed journals such as *Communication Monographs*, *Management Communication Quarterly*, the *Journal of Applied Communication Research*, and *Communication Studies*. For the last two decades he has consulted or spoken for the likes of Nike, Google, Visa, and the Center for Homeland Defense and Security. He hosts the 400,000+ subscriber YouTube channel Communication Coach and is the founder of Communication Coach Academy.